Front Office Procedure

Front Office Procedure refers to the standardized processes and practices that the front office staff in a hospitality setting, such as a hotel, follow to manage guest interactions from arrival to departure. This includes handling reservations, check-in and check-out processes, room allocation, billing, guest inquiries, and communication. The front office acts as the primary point of contact for guests, ensuring smooth service delivery and a positive guest experience. Key responsibilities involve maintaining records, managing guest accounts, addressing complaints, and coordinating with other departments like housekeeping and maintenance. Effective front office procedures are essential for efficient hotel operations, enhancing guest satisfaction and loyalty.

Elizabeth Jimenez

- Understanding types of reservations (individual, group, corporate)
- Reservation sources (direct, online, travel agents, etc.)
- Steps for handling reservations and confirming bookings
- Overbooking and handling of waitlisted guests

Chapter 4: Registration and Check-in Process

- Pre-arrival preparation and guest profiling
- Steps in the guest check-in process
- Different registration methods (manual, computerized, kiosk)
- Importance of welcoming the guest and creating a first impression

Chapter 5: Room Allocation and Assignment

- Types of rooms and room categorization
- Procedures for room assignment based on guest preferences
- Upgrading and upselling techniques
- Handling VIP and special guest accommodations

Chapter 6: Handling Guest Services

- Overview of concierge and guest services
- Assisting with transportation, dining, and local tours
- Handling guest inquiries and requests efficiently
- Protocols for special requests and amenities

Chapter 7: Guest Billing and Payment Procedures

- Types of payment methods accepted
- Understanding billing instructions and guest folios
- Processing payments and managing guest accounts
- Handling disputes and errors in billing

Chapter 8: Check-out and Departure Process

- Preparation for guest check-out
- Steps in the check-out process (settling accounts, issuing invoices)
- Handling feedback during check-out
- Farewell etiquette and follow-up actions

Chapter 9: Telephone Etiquette and Call Management

- Importance of professional telephone etiquette
- Handling guest calls, inquiries, and requests
- Managing multiple calls and prioritizing responses
- Techniques for handling difficult calls

Chapter 10: Guest Relations and Handling Complaints

- Importance of guest relations in front office operations
- Techniques for handling guest complaints and issues
- Building rapport and maintaining guest satisfaction
- Handling critical situations and guest recovery techniques

Chapter 11: Night Audit Procedures

- Purpose of the night audit and daily closure process
- Steps involved in the night audit process

- Generating daily reports and analyzing room occupancy
- Identifying and correcting errors in transactions

Chapter 12: Safety and Security in Front Office Operations

- Understanding guest safety and hotel security protocols
- Handling lost and found items
- Procedures for emergency situations (fire, medical, evacuation)
- Working with security staff and protocols for suspicious activities

Chapter 13: Role of Technology in Front Office

- Introduction to Property Management Systems (PMS)
- Utilizing front office software for efficiency
- Role of mobile apps and self-service kiosks
- Emerging trends in front office technology (AI, chatbots)

Chapter 14: Managing Front Office Staff

- Recruitment and training of front office staff

- Developing a customer-focused team
- Scheduling and managing shifts
- Importance of teamwork and leadership in the front office

Chapter 15: Revenue Management and Front Office

- Basics of revenue management in the front office
- Dynamic pricing and room rate strategies
- Techniques for maximizing occupancy and revenue
- Working with the sales team for group reservations

Chapter 16: Housekeeping Coordination with Front Office

- Importance of communication between front office and housekeeping
- Room status and occupancy coordination
- Handling guest room requests and special instructions
- Procedures for room inspections and readiness

Chapter 17: Marketing and Sales Coordination

- Role of the front office in marketing hotel services
- Promoting upsells and add-on services
- Handling VIP guests and loyalty programs
- Working with the sales department for promotional activities

Chapter 18: Guest Feedback and Service Improvement

- Collecting guest feedback (in-person, digital surveys)
- Analyzing guest feedback for service improvement
- Implementing changes based on guest insights
- Importance of continuous training and improvement

Chapter 19: Financial and Statistical Analysis for Front Office

- Key performance indicators (KPIs) for the front office

- Budgeting and forecasting for front office operations
- Analysis of occupancy and revenue statistics
- Reporting and documenting front office performance

Chapter 20: Front Office Trends and Future Outlook

- Trends in front office management and guest expectations
- Evolving role of front office with automation
- Environmental sustainability in front office operations
- Future of front office careers and skills development

ABOUT THE AUTHOR

Introducing Elizabeth Jimenez, a bright young newbie writer in the industry. Set off on a word adventure that captivates her expertise with a fresh perspective and a passion for writing a book relevant to her knowledge. Elizabeth Jimenez, a novice writer, captivates readers with her words by fusing genuineness with inventiveness. She promises a lovely escape and welcomes them to embark on an exciting writing journey. I appreciate your reading my works.

Chapter 1: Introduction to the Front Office Department

Definition and Role of the Front Office in a Hotel

The front office department is the hub of guest interaction and service within a hotel. Often referred to as the "*face*" of the hotel, the front office is the first and last point of contact for guests, playing a crucial role in shaping their overall experience. This department is responsible for welcoming guests, processing reservations, handling check-in and check-out, managing guest accounts, and addressing inquiries and complaints. It serves as the communication center for guests, directing them to various hotel services and ensuring they have a pleasant stay.

The front office staff works in close collaboration with other departments, such as housekeeping, maintenance, food and beverage, and security, to ensure seamless operations. By providing essential services with warmth, professionalism, and efficiency, the front office significantly influences guest satisfaction and the hotel's reputation. In many cases, guests perceive the quality of their stay based on their interactions with the front office team, making this department a key contributor to customer loyalty.

Organizational Structure and Roles within the Department

The front office department is typically organized into several key roles, each with specific responsibilities that contribute to the department's smooth functioning. In larger hotels, the department may be divided into various sections, while smaller hotels may combine some roles.

1. **Front Office Manager**: The front office manager oversees the entire department, ensuring that all operations are efficient, policies are followed, and guest expectations are met. This position involves scheduling,

training staff, handling escalated complaints, and ensuring the department aligns with the hotel's standards.

2. **Assistant Front Office Manager**: Reporting directly to the front office manager, the assistant manager helps in day-to-day operations and takes on managerial duties when the front office manager is unavailable. This role often includes supervising staff and helping handle challenging guest interactions.

3. **Guest Relations Officer (GRO)**: A Guest Relations Officer is responsible for creating a personalized experience for guests, often focusing on VIPs, loyalty program members, and returning guests. The GRO is the primary point of contact for handling special requests and managing high-value guests.

4. **Receptionist / Front Desk Agent**: Receptionists are the frontline staff who greet guests, handle check-ins and check-outs,

process payments, and manage guest queries. They play a pivotal role in establishing a welcoming atmosphere and addressing guest needs.

5. **Concierge**: The concierge provides guests with information about local attractions, transportation, and dining options. They also arrange reservations, tickets, and other external services, aiming to enhance the guest experience.

6. **Bell Staff / Porters**: Bell staff are responsible for assisting guests with their luggage, guiding them to their rooms, and providing information about room facilities. They work closely with the front desk to offer smooth service and ensure guests feel comfortable upon arrival.

7. **Night Auditor**: The night auditor performs accounting duties during night shifts, including closing the day's financial transactions and creating daily reports. This

role ensures that all accounts are balanced, allowing the next day to start smoothly.

8. **Reservation Agent**: Reservation agents handle booking inquiries, manage room availability, and confirm reservations. They liaise with various online travel agents and booking platforms to ensure accurate room allocation and pricing.

The organizational structure and division of duties help the front office run efficiently and ensure that guests receive consistent, high-quality service regardless of the time of day or night.

Key Responsibilities and Functions

The front office department performs a wide range of responsibilities that can be divided into core functions essential to daily operations:

1. **Reservations Management**: The front office team handles incoming reservations, confirming bookings, and ensuring room

availability. They coordinate with revenue management to maximize occupancy and often employ upselling techniques to increase hotel revenue.

2. **Guest Check-in and Check-out**: Managing guest arrivals and departures is a critical function of the front office. During check-in, staff confirm reservations, complete the registration process, allocate rooms, and inform guests of hotel amenities. At check-out, they process payments, handle invoices, and address any final questions or issues.

3. **Room Assignment**: Front office staff ensure that rooms are assigned according to guest preferences and hotel policies, factoring in special requests and upgrades when possible. Room assignment also involves liaising with housekeeping to ensure readiness.

4. **Billing and Payment Processing**: The front office team manages guest accounts, processes payments, and ensures accurate

billing for services used. This includes keeping track of all transactions, managing guest folios, and settling accounts at check-out.

5. **Handling Guest Inquiries and Complaints**: Guest inquiries about hotel services, local attractions, and special requests are directed to the front office, which is trained to provide clear, helpful responses. Staff also handle complaints, working to resolve issues swiftly and professionally to maintain a positive guest experience.

6. **Concierge Services**: The front office provides concierge services, helping guests with dining reservations, event tickets, transportation, and more. This service enhances the guest experience by offering personalized recommendations and assistance.

7. **Safety and Security Coordination**: The front office team plays a role in ensuring guest safety by following hotel security protocols, managing lost and found items, and coordinating with the security department in emergencies.

8. **Night Auditing**: Night auditors ensure that all financial records are accurate and that the day's transactions are balanced. They generate reports on occupancy, revenue, and expenses, which are used by management to make informed decisions.

9. **Communication and Coordination**: The front office coordinates with other hotel departments to meet guest needs. For example, they inform housekeeping of room status changes, alert maintenance of repair needs, and work with food and beverage for special requests.

These responsibilities require a high degree of organization, attention to detail, and excellent customer service skills to ensure efficient operations and guest satisfaction.

Importance of the Front Office for Guest Experience

The front office department is essential to creating a positive guest experience. As the first point of contact upon arrival, the front office sets the tone for the entire stay, establishing the initial impression of the hotel. A warm welcome and smooth check-in process can make guests feel valued and appreciated, while quick and efficient service during check-out leaves a lasting positive impression.

The front office team is trained to provide a range of services that make guests' stays comfortable and enjoyable. By handling requests, answering inquiries, and offering recommendations, they add value to the guest experience, making guests more likely to return and recommend the hotel to others.

The front office plays a crucial role in managing guest feedback and resolving complaints. By addressing issues professionally and finding quick solutions, the front office can turn potential negative experiences into positive ones, reinforcing guest loyalty and enhancing the hotel's reputation.

The front office is also vital to the hotel's revenue through its roles in reservations, upselling, and concierge services. A well-trained front office team can boost revenue by suggesting upgrades and promoting hotel amenities, contributing to the financial success of the property.

The front office department is not only the operational backbone of a hotel but also the primary driver of guest satisfaction. The professionalism, warmth, and efficiency of the front office team significantly influence how guests perceive the quality of their stay, making this department central to any hotel's success.

Chapter 2: Front Office Communication Skills

Effective communication is one of the most critical skills for front office staff in a hotel. As the first point of contact, the front office team shapes the guest's first impression and continues to impact the guest's experience throughout their stay. Whether it's in person, on the phone, or via digital channels, effective communication ensures guests feel valued, understood, and well-served. In addition to guest interactions, the front office also plays a central role in coordinating with other hotel departments to meet guest needs and handle operational demands smoothly.

Effective Communication with Guests

Guest satisfaction is highly influenced by the way front office staff communicate. Effective communication with guests involves:

1. **Warmth and Friendliness**: A smile, eye contact, and polite language can make guests feel welcome and valued. The goal is to create a positive first impression and establish a friendly rapport.

2. **Active Listening**: Listening attentively to guests allows staff to understand their needs and concerns fully. This means not interrupting, maintaining eye contact, and giving verbal or non-verbal cues to show understanding.

3. **Clarity and Conciseness**: Clear communication is essential to avoid misunderstandings. Staff should use simple language, avoid jargon, and confirm that the guest understands any instructions, especially regarding hotel policies, billing, or directions.

4. **Empathy and Patience**: Communicating with empathy is crucial, particularly when dealing with complaints or distressed guests. Showing that the hotel cares about the guest's

experience fosters trust and can defuse tense situations.

5. **Personalization**: Addressing guests by their names, acknowledging past stays, or referring to specific preferences enhances communication. Personal touches help guests feel valued and recognized, fostering a positive experience.

By mastering these communication techniques, front office staff can enhance guest satisfaction, foster loyalty, and contribute to the hotel's positive reputation.

Telephone and In-Person Communication Protocols

The front office team must be skilled in both telephone and in-person communication, as each requires a unique approach to meet professional standards and guest expectations.

1. **Telephone Communication**:

o **Answering Promptly**: Calls should be answered within a few rings to show attentiveness. This is especially important as guests often call to address urgent needs.

o **Using a Friendly Greeting**: A warm greeting, including the hotel name and the staff member's name, sets a polite and professional tone.

o **Active Listening and Clear Responses**: Staff should listen carefully, confirm understanding, and provide clear answers. If they need to put the guest on hold, they should ask for permission and explain why.

o **Taking Notes**: During phone conversations, it's essential to take notes to avoid missing details, particularly for complaints, special requests, or room service orders.

- o **Closing with Courtesy**: Ending calls with phrases like *"Thank you for calling. We look forward to welcoming you soon!"* reinforces professionalism.

2. **In-Person Communication**:

   - o **Creating a Warm Welcome**: Upon entering the hotel, guests expect a warm, genuine greeting. Staff should make eye contact, smile, and offer assistance immediately.

   - o **Professional Body Language**: In-person communication is as much non-verbal as it is verbal. Staff should maintain an open, approachable posture and avoid actions that could convey disinterest or impatience, such as looking at their phone or clock.

   - o **Positive and Polite Language**: When responding to guest inquiries, positive language should be used to reassure guests. Instead of saying, *"I can't help with that,"* say, *"Let me find someone who can assist you with that."*

- ○ **Closing with Gratitude**: When concluding in-person interactions, thanking the guest and expressing a wish for them to enjoy their stay shows appreciation and encourages positive feedback.

Effective telephone and in-person protocols are fundamental to maintaining a professional atmosphere and ensuring guest satisfaction.

Handling Guest Complaints and Requests Professionally

Guests may occasionally experience issues or make special requests that require extra care and professionalism from front office staff. When these situations arise, the way staff handle them can turn a negative situation into a positive guest experience.

1. **Listen and Show Empathy**: Staff should let the guest explain the issue fully without interruption, demonstrating empathy through body language and verbal cues. Saying, *"I understand how this might be frustrating for you,"* shows compassion.

2. **Take Ownership and Apologize**: Regardless of the cause of the issue, front office staff should take ownership of the situation on behalf of the hotel and offer a sincere apology. For example, *"I'm sorry for the inconvenience you've experienced. Let me take care of this for you."*

3. **Find Solutions**: Whenever possible, front office staff should be empowered to offer solutions, whether it's arranging a room change, providing complimentary services, or involving a manager for higher-level issues.

4. **Follow Up**: For significant complaints or requests, staff should follow up to ensure the

issue has been resolved to the guest's satisfaction. This may involve calling the guest's room, sending a message, or leaving a note.

5. **Stay Calm and Professional**: Front office staff must maintain professionalism even if a guest becomes upset. Staying calm helps defuse tension and allows the guest to feel heard.

Handling complaints and requests with professionalism helps maintain a positive guest experience, enhances the hotel's reputation, and demonstrates the hotel's commitment to service excellence.

Cross-Departmental Communication and Coordination

Effective communication within the front office is critical, but equally important is the ability to coordinate seamlessly with other hotel departments, including housekeeping, maintenance, food and beverage, and security. This collaboration ensures that guest needs are met efficiently and that hotel operations run smoothly.

1. **Housekeeping**:

   o **Room Readiness and Turnover**: Communication between the front office and housekeeping is vital for room status updates. Housekeeping must inform the front office when rooms are ready for check-in, while the front office notifies housekeeping about expected check-outs and any room cleaning requests.

   o **Special Requests**: If guests request additional amenities or specific cleaning services, the front office relays these to housekeeping to ensure they are met.

2. **Maintenance**:

- ○ **Reporting Issues**: If a guest reports a maintenance problem, the front office must communicate this to the maintenance team promptly. This includes issues like broken fixtures, air conditioning problems, or other in-room issues.

- ○ **Coordinating Repairs**: For rooms undergoing repairs, the front office should know when maintenance is completed to update room status accordingly.

3. **Food and Beverage**:

- ○ **Guest Orders and Room Service**: When guests order room service, the front office may need to coordinate with the food and beverage department, particularly for billing or special requests.

- o **Promoting F&B Services**: The front office staff often provide information on hotel dining options and may make reservations, requiring regular communication with the F&B team.

4. **Security**:

   - o **Emergency Situations**: During emergencies, such as fire alarms, medical incidents, or security concerns, the front office must work closely with security to follow established protocols and ensure guest safety.

   - o **Handling Lost and Found**: Security and the front office coordinate to manage lost and found items, ensuring guests' belongings are kept secure and can be returned to them promptly.

5. **Sales and Events**:

- o **Guest Bookings and Events**: The front office often coordinates with the sales department to manage group bookings, event attendees, and special arrangements.

- o **Promoting Hotel Amenities**: Cross-departmental communication helps the front office stay informed about ongoing promotions or events so that they can relay this information to guests.

By fostering strong communication channels across departments, the front office ensures that guest needs are met promptly and that the hotel functions as a cohesive unit. This cooperation ultimately enhances the guest experience by reducing wait times, streamlining operations, and delivering high-quality service.

Effective communication skills are essential to the success of the front office department. From engaging warmly with guests to managing complaints and coordinating with other hotel departments, each aspect of communication contributes to a positive guest experience and smooth hotel operations.

Chapter 3: Guest Reservation Process

The reservation process is one of the most fundamental aspects of front office operations, as it is the first step in building a relationship with the guest. The reservation process not only ensures that guests have accommodations ready for them but also allows hotels to manage occupancy, pricing, and room allocation efficiently. This chapter covers the different types of reservations, the sources through which reservations are received, the step-by-step process for handling reservations, and strategies for managing overbooking and waitlisted guests.

Understanding Types of Reservations

Reservations vary based on the type of guest or booking party and can be classified into several categories:

1. **Individual Reservations**:

   o These are bookings made by individual travelers or small parties, often for personal travel. Individual reservations can be made directly through the hotel or via online channels.

   o Individual travelers often book for leisure, business, or short-term stays, and their needs can be met without extensive arrangements or customizations.

2. **Group Reservations**:

   o Group reservations involve multiple rooms booked under a single reservation for a common purpose, such as a conference, wedding, or tour group. These reservations often require special handling, coordination, and, in many cases, a group discount.

o Hotels benefit from group bookings as they can quickly fill up multiple rooms and secure revenue in advance. However, groups may have special needs, such as meeting rooms, meal arrangements, or early check-ins.

3. **Corporate Reservations**:

o Corporate reservations are made on behalf of employees or executives by companies for business-related travel. These reservations are often part of a corporate account with the hotel, involving negotiated rates and other contractual arrangements.

o Corporate clients typically expect consistency in service, efficiency during check-in/out, and flexible billing options. They may also have access to additional amenities like business centers or meeting rooms.

Each type of reservation comes with specific expectations and arrangements, and understanding these helps the front office tailor the booking and service experience accordingly.

Reservation Sources

Guests make reservations through a variety of channels. The reservation source affects how bookings are processed, how revenue is managed, and the availability of information for personalization.

1. **Direct Reservations**:

   o Direct reservations are made when guests contact the hotel directly, whether through phone, email, the hotel's website, or in person.

   o These reservations are preferred by many hotels because they avoid third-party fees and allow for direct communication, making it easier to personalize service and build guest loyalty.

2. **Online Travel Agencies (OTAs)**:

   o OTAs like Booking.com, Expedia, and Agoda are third-party platforms that allow travelers to browse and book accommodations online. These platforms offer guests access to a variety of options but charge hotels a commission for each booking.

   o While OTAs provide hotels with broad exposure and access to a wider audience, they also limit direct interaction with the guest until after booking.

3. **Global Distribution Systems (GDS)**:

o GDS platforms, such as Amadeus, Sabre, and Galileo, are used by travel agents and corporate clients to book hotels alongside flights and car rentals.

o These systems are integral for corporate and group travel as they offer real-time availability across multiple services, but hotels pay a fee for each GDS booking.

4. **Travel Agents**:

o Traditional travel agents book accommodations on behalf of their clients, often in collaboration with specific hotels that offer commission incentives. These agents can handle reservations for both individuals and groups, adding a layer of personalized service.

o Travel agents are commonly used for complex itineraries, luxury travel, and by clients who prefer a high-touch service experience.

5. **Mobile Apps and Self-Booking Platforms**:

   o Many guests now prefer to book directly via mobile apps or digital platforms that allow quick, convenient access to reservations.

   o Mobile bookings appeal especially to younger guests and last-minute travelers, and hotels are increasingly investing in app-based solutions to cater to this market.

Understanding the various sources of reservations helps the front office staff manage booking requests more efficiently and allocate resources according to the demand from each channel.

Steps for Handling Reservations and Confirming Bookings

The reservation process includes a series of standardized steps designed to ensure accurate bookings and clear communication with the guest. Here are the typical steps:

1. **Receiving the Reservation Request**:

   o The front office receives reservation requests through one of the channels mentioned above. Details like guest name, contact information, check-in and check-out dates, room type, and any special requests are collected.

2. **Checking Availability**:

   o The front office staff checks room availability based on the guest's requirements and hotel occupancy forecasts. If the requested room type is not available, they may offer alternative options or suggest different dates.

3. **Confirming the Reservation Details**:

○ Once availability is confirmed, staff confirm the reservation details with the guest, including room rate, payment method, and cancellation policies. For group or corporate reservations, additional details like billing arrangements and special services are noted.

4. **Recording the Reservation in the Property Management System (PMS):**

○ The reservation details are entered into the hotel's PMS. This ensures that all information is recorded accurately and can be accessed by relevant departments. It also allows the hotel to track occupancy and revenue metrics.

5. **Sending Confirmation to the Guest:**

○ A reservation confirmation is sent to the guest, usually via email. This includes essential details like the booking reference number, room type, rates, check-in/check-out times, and hotel contact information. For group or corporate bookings, special instructions or services are confirmed as well.

6. **Pre-Arrival Preparation**:

  o For VIP guests or guests with specific preferences, the front office may prepare in advance, informing relevant departments of any special requests. This stage allows the hotel to deliver a more personalized experience upon check-in.

Proper handling of reservations minimizes the risk of errors, ensures a smooth check-in process, and enhances the guest experience.

Overbooking and Handling of Waitlisted Guests

Overbooking is a common practice in the hotel industry used to maximize revenue and occupancy.

Hotels may slightly overbook to account for cancellations or no-shows. However, if all guests show up as scheduled, the front office must manage the situation with professionalism to maintain guest satisfaction.

1. **Understanding Overbooking**:

   o Overbooking involves accepting more reservations than the available rooms to compensate for potential cancellations and no-shows. Hotels often use historical data and industry practices to predict safe overbooking levels. While it is profitable, overbooking can lead to uncomfortable situations if not managed carefully.

2. **Handling Waitlisted Guests**:

   o In cases where the hotel is fully booked, guests may be placed on a waitlist. Front office staff manage waitlisted guests by recording their contact information and informing them if rooms become available.

- o Waitlisted guests are prioritized based on factors like loyalty program membership, reservation source, and time of booking.

3. **Dealing with Overbooked Guests on Arrival**:

- o If a guest arrives and no rooms are available due to overbooking, the hotel may offer alternative accommodations. This process, known as *"walking"* a guest, involves arranging and often paying for a room at a nearby hotel of similar quality.

- o Staff should apologize sincerely, offer a solution, and ensure the guest's transportation to the new location. Some hotels may also offer additional compensation, like complimentary future stays or amenities, to retain guest loyalty.

4. **Communication with Guests**:

   o Transparency is key in handling overbooking situations. Hotels should communicate potential overbooking outcomes to guests in advance, if possible, to manage expectations. If a guest must be *"walked,"* staff should handle the conversation empathetically and professionally.

5. **Post-Stay Follow-Up**:

   o Following up with guests who were affected by overbooking shows that the hotel values their satisfaction. A personalized apology, along with any compensation, can help restore goodwill and increase the chances of the guest returning in the future.

Proper management of overbooking and waitlisted guests minimizes negative experiences, protects the hotel's reputation, and demonstrates a commitment to guest satisfaction.

The reservation process is fundamental to a hotel's success. It not only ensures the efficient management of room inventory but also provides opportunities to personalize the guest experience. By understanding the types and sources of reservations, handling booking requests professionally, and managing overbookings effectively, the front office can contribute significantly to guest satisfaction, operational efficiency, and revenue growth.

Chapter 4: Registration and Check-In Process

The registration and check-in process mark the official start of a guest's stay and is a critical point of interaction that shapes their first impression of the hotel. This chapter delves into the pre-arrival preparations and guest profiling, the essential steps involved in the check-in process, the different registration methods used, and the significance of welcoming the guest warmly.

Pre-Arrival Preparation and Guest Profiling

Preparing for a guest's arrival begins long before they walk through the hotel doors. Pre-arrival preparation and guest profiling are essential steps that allow front office staff to anticipate needs and personalize the experience, enhancing guest satisfaction.

1. **Guest Profiling**:

   o Profiling involves gathering and organizing information about the guest's preferences, past stays, and any special requests. This can include room type preferences, preferred amenities, special dietary needs, or loyalty program status.

- o Information from guest profiles helps front office staff personalize interactions, making the guest feel recognized and valued. For example, if a guest always requests a high-floor room, the front desk can ensure this preference is accommodated.

2. **Room Allocation and Preparation**:

- o Based on the guest profile, front office staff pre-assign a room that meets the guest's requirements. VIP guests, for example, may be assigned suites, and families with children may be placed near amenities such as pools or recreational areas.

- o The front office team coordinates with housekeeping to ensure the room is clean and ready upon arrival. Any special requests, such as extra pillows or specific amenities, are arranged beforehand.

3. **Welcome Amenities**:

   o For VIPs or loyal guests, the hotel may prepare welcome amenities such as a fruit basket, a handwritten note, or complimentary treats. This gesture enhances the guest's arrival experience and sets a positive tone for their stay.

By preparing for the guest's arrival in advance, the hotel demonstrates attentiveness and professionalism, laying the groundwork for a memorable experience.

Steps in the Guest Check-In Process

The check-in process involves a series of structured steps that ensure accuracy, efficiency, and a welcoming experience. Each step plays a role in creating a smooth and positive check-in for the guest.

1. **Greeting and Welcoming**:

   o A friendly greeting and warm welcome set the tone for the guest's stay. The front desk staff should address the guest by name, smile, and make eye contact. Welcoming gestures, such as offering a beverage or assisting with luggage, enhance the guest's comfort and sense of hospitality.

2. **Confirmation of Reservation Details**:

   o Front desk staff verify the reservation details with the guest, including check-in and check-out dates, room type, and any special requests. Confirming these details helps prevent misunderstandings and allows the guest to address any last-minute needs.

3. **Registration and Documentation**:

o The registration process typically involves filling out or confirming personal information, contact details, and payment methods. For hotels that require additional verification, such as passports or ID cards, staff will request and copy these documents.

o Many hotels now use digital registration methods that allow guests to complete these forms on tablets or via self-check-in kiosks.

4. **Assigning the Room and Issuing the Key**:

o Once registration is complete, the front desk staff assigns a room to the guest and issues room keys or access cards. For security, staff should explain how to use the key card and confirm the room number discreetly.

o Staff should offer to provide directions to the room and may suggest bell service assistance for luggage.

5. **Explaining Hotel Facilities and Amenities**:

o The front desk team provides information on hotel facilities, such as restaurants, fitness centers, pools, and any available events or activities. They should also highlight any guest-specific amenities, such as complimentary breakfasts or welcome drinks.

o Mentioning the availability of additional services, like concierge or room service, and explaining the check-out process helps ensure guests feel oriented.

6. **Confirming Payment and Authorization**:

o Before finalizing check-in, the front office may require a credit card authorization or deposit to cover incidental charges. Guests should be informed clearly about the amount being held and the hotel's policies on additional expenses.

7. **Offering Assistance and Final Farewell**:

   o Before the guest proceeds to their room, the front office team should ask if they need any additional assistance or have questions. Concluding the check-in with a warm farewell reinforces a positive first impression and signals the start of a pleasant stay.

Following these steps ensures that check-in is thorough, welcoming, and leaves a positive impression on the guest.

Different Registration Methods (Manual, Computerized, Kiosk)

Hotels use various methods to complete the registration process, depending on the property's size, available technology, and guest preferences. Here are the primary registration methods:

1. **Manual Registration**:

   o This traditional method involves physical paperwork and is commonly used in smaller or boutique hotels where personalized service is a priority. Guests fill out a registration form by hand, and front desk staff manually record the information.

   o While this method can be time-consuming, it allows for personalized guest interactions. It may be preferred by guests who value high-touch service over efficiency.

2. **Computerized Registration**:

   o In computerized registration, front office staff enter guest details into a Property Management System (PMS), which automates room assignments, billing, and guest profiles. Computerized systems allow for quick data entry, accurate record-keeping, and integration with other hotel departments.

o This is the most widely used registration method in modern hotels, as it provides efficiency and access to guest data for personalized service.

3. **Self-Check-In Kiosks and Mobile Check-In**:

o Many hotels now offer self-check-in kiosks or mobile check-in options, allowing guests to check in independently. Kiosks are often available in the lobby and are particularly popular in business and airport hotels where guests may prioritize speed and efficiency.

- Mobile check-in enables guests to use a mobile app to complete registration, access their room via a digital key, and even check out. This method appeals to tech-savvy guests who prefer contactless services.

Each registration method has its advantages, and hotels may offer multiple options to cater to different guest preferences.

Importance of Welcoming the Guest and Creating a First Impression

The check-in experience is often a guest's first in-person interaction with the hotel, and first impressions are lasting. A warm, professional welcome can set a positive tone for the guest's stay, establishing a sense of trust and comfort.

1. **Building Trust and Loyalty**:

   - A friendly, attentive greeting signals that the hotel values the guest's presence and is ready to meet their needs. Staff should use the guest's name, acknowledge any special requests, and ensure that the guest feels welcomed.

o Creating a strong first impression can foster guest loyalty, increasing the likelihood of repeat visits and positive reviews.

2. **Demonstrating Professionalism and Hospitality**:

o Guests expect the hotel staff to be competent, polite, and helpful. A smooth check-in demonstrates the hotel's organizational skills and commitment to service excellence, which influences the guest's perception of the property.

o Professionalism at check-in extends beyond basic courtesy; it includes efficiency in handling documents, providing accurate information, and ensuring all guest needs are anticipated.

3. **Personalizing the Experience**:

   o When the front desk staff takes time to address the guest's preferences and needs, it creates a personalized experience that makes the guest feel valued. Small gestures, such as acknowledging a guest's birthday or anniversary, go a long way in creating memorable experiences.

   o Personalized service builds emotional connections, setting the hotel apart from competitors and enhancing guest satisfaction.

4. **Setting the Tone for the Entire Stay**:

   o The check-in process sets the stage for the rest of the guest's experience. If guests feel welcomed and well-informed upon arrival, they are more likely to overlook minor issues during their stay and feel comfortable asking for assistance when needed.

○ A positive check-in experience contributes to the overall guest satisfaction and creates a solid foundation for future interactions with the hotel.

The registration and check-in process is more than just a formality; it is an opportunity to establish a connection with the guest, showcase the hotel's professionalism, and deliver an exceptional first impression. By prioritizing guest needs, personalizing interactions, and ensuring efficiency, the front office team creates a welcoming environment that sets the stage for a memorable stay.

Chapter 5: Room Allocation and Assignment

Room allocation and assignment are critical tasks within the front office department that impact the guest experience and maximize room occupancy and revenue. This chapter covers the types of rooms and room categories commonly found in hotels, procedures for room assignment based on guest preferences, techniques for upgrading and upselling, and special handling of VIP and other high-profile guests.

Types of Rooms and Room Categorization

Hotels offer a variety of room types and categories to cater to the diverse preferences and budgets of guests. Understanding these categories helps the front office match guests with suitable accommodations and provide accurate information during the booking and check-in processes.

1. **Basic Room Types**:

     o **Single Room**: Accommodates one person, usually with a single bed, often preferred by solo travelers or business guests.

o **Double Room**: Designed for two people, typically with one double bed or two twin beds. Popular among couples and friends traveling together.

o **Twin Room**: Features two separate beds, accommodating two guests. Often chosen by guests who prefer separate sleeping arrangements.

o **Suite**: A larger, more luxurious accommodation, often with a separate living area, bedroom, and sometimes a kitchenette. Suites are ideal for VIPs, business executives, or families.

o **Family Room**: Specifically designed for families, often larger in size and with multiple beds to accommodate parents and children.

2. Specialty Rooms:

- **Connecting Rooms**: Rooms with a shared internal door, allowing guests to move between rooms. These are popular among families and groups.

- **Accessible Rooms**: Rooms with design features that cater to guests with disabilities, such as wheelchair-accessible showers, lower bed heights, and grab bars.

- **Executive Rooms**: Typically located on higher floors or *"executive levels,"* offering upgraded amenities and access to exclusive facilities like business lounges.

3. Categorization by View and Amenities:

- **Ocean/Sea View Room**: A room with a view of the sea, often more expensive than rooms without a view.

- **Garden/City View Room**: Rooms with pleasant views of gardens, cityscapes, or hotel courtyards.

- **Club or Concierge Floor Rooms**: Rooms on exclusive floors with added amenities, personalized services, and sometimes access to a private lounge.

Room categories allow hotels to target different market segments and help front desk staff make accurate room assignments based on guest needs and preferences.

Procedures for Room Assignment Based on Guest Preferences

The room assignment process involves matching available rooms to guests' preferences and requirements. This task requires careful coordination and often involves balancing room availability, guest expectations, and hotel policies.

1. **Reviewing Guest Preferences**:

o Upon arrival or during the booking process, front office staff should review any guest preferences, such as high-floor rooms, quiet zones, or specific bed types. This information may come from the guest's profile or loyalty program, providing insight into their past preferences.

2. **Room Availability and Assignment**:

o Using the Property Management System (PMS), front office staff check room availability and pre-assign rooms based on the guest's requirements. Staff may reserve certain rooms in advance for VIPs or guests with special needs.

o Room blocking is used to ensure rooms are set aside for specific guests, based on their requirements. For example, if a guest requested a non-smoking room or one close to the elevator, blocking ensures the room is allocated accordingly.

3. **Balancing Occupancy Levels**:

   o Room assignment decisions are made with an eye toward maximizing occupancy and minimizing room changes. Staff avoid assigning back-to-back stays in adjacent rooms when possible, reducing wear and tear and ensuring flexibility in room availability.

4. **Coordinating with Housekeeping**:

   o Housekeeping plays a key role in room assignment, as rooms must be cleaned and prepared before guests arrive. Communication between the front office and housekeeping ensures rooms are ready on time and avoids assigning rooms under cleaning or maintenance.

Room assignment requires attentiveness to detail, efficient communication, and prioritization to align guest needs with hotel resources.

Upgrading and Upselling Techniques

The check-in process offers a valuable opportunity to upgrade and upsell room options, enhancing guest satisfaction while generating additional revenue for the hotel.

1. **Identifying Upgrade Opportunities**:

    o Upgrading involves moving a guest from their reserved room category to a higher category, usually at no additional charge. Front office staff may upgrade guests with loyalty status, VIPs, or those celebrating special occasions.

    o Complimentary upgrades can improve guest loyalty and leave a positive impression, making guests more likely to return or recommend the hotel.

2. Upselling Techniques:

- Upselling involves offering a higher room category for an additional fee. Front office staff can highlight the benefits of upgraded rooms, such as larger space, better views, or exclusive amenities, to encourage guests to consider these options.

- Effective upselling relies on understanding guest needs. For example, a couple on a romantic getaway might be interested in a room with a view, while a business traveler might appreciate an executive suite with office amenities.

3. Using Promotional Packages:

- Hotels often create packages that combine room upgrades with amenities, such as spa access or dining credits. Front office staff can promote these packages as a way to enhance the guest experience at a discounted rate.

4. **Timing and Presentation**:

   o Front office staff should present upgrade and upsell options casually and respectfully, emphasizing the benefits rather than pressuring the guest. Timing is key; it's best to offer these options early in the check-in process before the guest has settled into a specific choice.

   Upselling and upgrading provide the hotel with opportunities to generate additional revenue while offering guests a more enjoyable experience.

Handling VIP and Special Guest Accommodations

VIP and special guest accommodations are managed with extra care to ensure a high level of service and personalization. VIPs, corporate executives, celebrities, or guests with special needs often require special handling to meet their expectations.

1. **VIP Guest Identification and Preparation**:

   o VIP guests are often identified before arrival through reservation notes or loyalty program memberships. Front office staff ensure that room assignments, welcome amenities, and special requests are prepared in advance.

   o VIP guests might receive additional amenities like complimentary beverages, personalized notes, or room upgrades. Some hotels create detailed profiles for VIPs, ensuring consistency in service during each stay.

2. **Privacy and Discretion**:

- o Special guests, especially public figures or celebrities, may require additional privacy and discretion. Staff are trained to avoid disclosing personal information and to handle requests with the utmost confidentiality.

- o Front desk staff may arrange for private check-ins and use aliases to protect the guest's privacy. Housekeeping and security are also informed of any special protocols for VIP guests.

3. **Room Customization and Special Amenities**:

- o For guests with specific requirements, such as allergies or disabilities, rooms are customized to meet their needs. This can include hypoallergenic linens, accessible bathroom features, or specific in-room amenities.

o VIPs and long-stay guests may have personalized amenities, such as preferred beverages or customized minibars, which add to their comfort and create a memorable experience.

4. **Coordinating with Other Departments**:

o Handling special guest accommodations often requires cross-departmental collaboration. For instance, the concierge team might assist in booking excursions, while housekeeping may provide additional turndown services.

o Communication between departments ensures that every aspect of the guest's stay is well-coordinated and meets high expectations.

Special handling of VIPs and guests with unique requirements showcases the hotel's commitment to guest satisfaction, creating lasting loyalty and a reputation for exceptional service.

Room allocation and assignment are vital aspects of the front office's role in enhancing the guest experience and optimizing room occupancy. By understanding room categories, following proper assignment procedures, effectively upselling and upgrading, and meeting the needs of VIPs, the front office team plays an instrumental role in delivering personalized service and maximizing hotel revenue.

Chapter 6: Handling Guest Services

Guest services play a significant role in enhancing the overall guest experience by providing assistance, information, and personalized care throughout the stay. This chapter provides an overview of the various concierge and guest services offered by hotels, methods for assisting with transportation, dining, and local tours, approaches for handling guest inquiries and requests efficiently, and protocols for managing special requests and amenities.

Overview of Concierge and Guest Services

The concierge and guest services team serve as the main point of contact for guests seeking assistance beyond the basics of room accommodations. Their primary responsibilities are to cater to guests' needs, answer questions, and provide valuable information that improves the guest's experience.

1. **Concierge Services**:

    o The concierge is often positioned in the hotel lobby and serves as an expert on the local area, offering assistance with recommendations and arrangements for dining, entertainment, transportation, and sightseeing.

    o Common services include securing dinner reservations, arranging transportation, booking tickets to shows or events, organizing tours, and providing information on local attractions. Concierges often possess deep knowledge of the area and maintain relationships with local vendors to offer exclusive experiences or special rates.

2. **Guest Services**:

- Guest services encompass a range of requests that contribute to guest comfort and convenience, such as handling luggage, providing wake-up calls, and arranging in-room services like dining or housekeeping.

- This team also addresses inquiries about hotel facilities, assists with additional needs such as extra linens or amenities, and handles any special requests the guest may have.

3. **Role of the Guest Services Team in Enhancing Guest Satisfaction**:

o The concierge and guest services team have a direct impact on guest satisfaction by going above and beyond standard service offerings, creating a personalized experience, and responding promptly to requests.

o Excellent guest service contributes to positive guest reviews, increases loyalty, and can often lead to referrals and return bookings. Effective guest service requires a combination of professionalism, attentiveness, and efficiency.

By maintaining a high standard of service and adapting to guests' individual needs, the concierge and guest services team builds lasting relationships with guests and enhances the hotel's reputation.

Assisting with Transportation, Dining, and Local Tours

Concierge and guest services often involve helping guests arrange transportation, dining experiences, and tours, which are essential parts of many travelers' itineraries. By efficiently handling these needs, the team makes the guest experience seamless and enjoyable.

1. **Transportation Assistance**:

   o **Airport Transfers**: Many hotels provide shuttle services or private transportation options to and from the airport. The guest services team arranges these transfers based on the guest's arrival and departure times, ensuring a smooth transition between the hotel and airport.

   o **Local Transportation**: Concierge staff may assist guests in renting cars, arranging taxis, or scheduling rides with trusted drivers. For guests looking to explore the city, they can also provide information on public transit options.

○ **Special Transportation Requests**: For VIPs or guests on special occasions, the concierge can arrange luxury transportation, such as limousines or private chauffeur services.

2. **Dining Reservations and Recommendations**:

○ **Restaurant Recommendations**: Concierge staff are often knowledgeable about local restaurants and can offer recommendations that match the guest's preferences, dietary restrictions, and budget.

○ **Making Reservations**: If a guest requests a reservation, the concierge will coordinate with the restaurant and secure a suitable table, often accommodating specific requests, like window seating or quiet areas. They may also work with restaurant managers to ensure availability, especially for last-minute requests.

- o **In-Room Dining and Catering**: For guests preferring to dine in their rooms, guest services can coordinate with the hotel's in-room dining team to deliver meals promptly. For special occasions or group events, they can also arrange private dining or catering services.

3. **Arranging Local Tours and Excursions**:

- o **Tour Bookings**: The concierge assists guests in booking tours of local attractions, such as historical landmarks, city tours, or adventure activities like hiking and water sports.

- o **Personalized Itineraries**: For guests with specific interests, the concierge may create customized itineraries or arrange for private guided tours. This service is especially valuable for international visitors unfamiliar with the area.

- **Coordination with Tour Operators**: The concierge maintains relationships with reputable tour operators, ensuring guests have safe, enjoyable experiences. This also allows the hotel to offer exclusive packages or discounts on popular activities.

By assisting with these arrangements, the guest services team ensures guests have memorable and well-organized experiences beyond the hotel, contributing to a positive overall impression.

Handling Guest Inquiries and Requests Efficiently

Efficiently handling guest inquiries and requests is essential for creating a smooth and enjoyable guest experience. This requires attentiveness, clear communication, and a proactive approach to meeting guest needs.

1. **Prompt and Courteous Responses**:

   o The guest services team should respond promptly to inquiries, demonstrating respect for the guest's time. Whether in person, over the phone, or through messaging platforms, a courteous and friendly tone creates a welcoming environment.

   o Even when the team cannot immediately fulfill a request, keeping the guest informed and offering estimated times for resolution helps maintain satisfaction.

2. **Understanding the Nature of the Request**:

o Guest services staff must listen carefully to understand the specifics of each request and clarify any details if needed. This ensures that the response is accurate and that expectations are met.

o Some requests, such as room changes or complaints, may require additional coordination with other departments. Proper communication ensures smooth handling without delays or miscommunications.

3. **Using Technology for Efficiency**:

o Many hotels use Property Management Systems (PMS) and communication platforms to log and track guest requests. This ensures requests are followed up on time and allows staff to access guest preferences for future interactions.

o Automated messaging systems, such as in-room tablets or hotel apps, also enable guests to make requests and inquiries quickly, enhancing response times and streamlining service.

4. **Anticipating and Proactively Addressing Guest Needs**:

o Beyond responding to direct requests, the guest services team can often anticipate needs based on guest profiles or patterns. For example, business travelers may appreciate early check-in options or a quiet workspace.

o Proactive service creates a seamless experience for guests, allowing them to enjoy their stay without needing to request each service individually.

Handling guest requests promptly, accurately, and with a positive attitude directly impacts guest satisfaction, fostering a sense of care and attentiveness.

Protocols for Special Requests and Amenities

Certain guest requests, such as arranging for special amenities or fulfilling unique preferences, require additional coordination and attention to detail. By following established protocols, the guest services team ensures a consistent and high-quality experience for all guests.

1. **Understanding Special Requests**:

    o Special requests might include additional amenities (like extra towels or pillows), dietary accommodations, allergy-friendly rooms, or specific arrangements for celebrations, such as birthdays or anniversaries.

    o Front desk staff should document these requests carefully and communicate them to the appropriate departments, such as housekeeping or food and beverage, to ensure they are fulfilled promptly.

2. **Special Occasion Arrangements**:

   o For occasions like anniversaries or birthdays, the guest services team may arrange for celebratory touches, such as a bottle of champagne, a custom cake, or floral arrangements.

   o For VIPs or guests celebrating significant milestones, the hotel may offer complimentary upgrades or special welcome amenities. These gestures create memorable experiences and enhance guest loyalty.

3. **Handling Special Needs and Accessibility Requests**:

   o Guests with disabilities or special needs often require specific room features, such as wheelchair accessibility, grab bars in the bathroom, or roll-in showers. The guest services team coordinates these requests with housekeeping and maintenance to prepare the room accordingly.

o Staff are trained to be respectful and discreet, ensuring guests feel comfortable and welcomed without drawing undue attention to their requirements.

4. **Coordinating Amenities with External Vendors**:

o For services that cannot be provided directly by the hotel, such as arranging a spa treatment at a nearby facility or securing tickets to a show, the concierge coordinates with trusted local vendors. This ensures guests receive quality service that meets the hotel's standards.

o By partnering with reputable providers, hotels can also offer exclusive access or discounts, adding value to the guest experience.

5. **Handling Unusual or Last-Minute Requests**:

o Some guest requests may be unusual or made at the last minute, such as requesting a particular room layout or organizing a last-minute celebration. In these cases, the guest services team should do their best to accommodate the request within the hotel's resources and policies.

o For high-profile or VIP guests, even challenging requests are often handled with flexibility to maintain the hotel's reputation for top-tier service.

By following these protocols, the guest services team can manage special requests efficiently and maintain a high standard of service that accommodates diverse guest needs.

The guest services team is essential to a hotel's ability to provide exceptional service, handling a variety of tasks that enhance guest satisfaction and ensure a smooth experience. From arranging transportation and dining to managing special requests and amenities, this team supports the guest's needs, demonstrates the hotel's commitment to service excellence, and contributes to a positive, memorable stay.

Chapter 7: Guest Billing and Payment Procedures

Billing and payment procedures are a core responsibility of the front office, ensuring that all financial transactions between the guest and hotel are handled accurately, transparently, and efficiently. In this chapter, we cover the types of payment methods typically accepted in hotels, how to understand billing instructions and guest folios, the process for managing guest accounts, and best practices for handling disputes or errors in billing.

Types of Payment Methods Accepted

Hotels offer a range of payment options to accommodate the preferences and convenience of guests. Front office staff must be well-versed in these options and knowledgeable about processing each one securely and accurately.

1. **Cash**:

   o Cash is often accepted for small transactions or as a method of settling final bills. However, for security reasons, many hotels prefer electronic payments over large cash payments.

   o Cash payments are often recorded in the guest's folio immediately, with receipts provided for both the guest and hotel's records.

2. **Credit and Debit Cards**:

   o Credit and debit cards are the most widely accepted forms of payment. Hotels typically require a credit card at check-in to authorize a certain amount for anticipated charges, including room rates, taxes, and potential incidental expenses.

   o Major credit cards such as Visa, MasterCard, American Express, and Discover are commonly accepted, and staff must verify the card's authenticity and the guest's identification for security.

3. **Mobile Payments**:

   o With the rise of mobile payment options like Apple Pay, Google Pay, and other digital wallets, many hotels now offer contactless payment options. These options allow guests to use their smartphones or other digital devices to make secure payments without needing physical cards or cash.

o Mobile payments are especially popular among younger travelers and are convenient for speeding up the check-in and check-out process.

4. **Bank Transfers and Electronic Funds Transfer (EFT):**

o Bank transfers or EFTs are often used for corporate bookings, group reservations, or long-term stays. In these cases, companies or booking agencies may arrange direct payments to the hotel.

o Hotels typically request proof of payment from the guest or the company prior to check-in to ensure the funds are received.

5. **Third-Party Billing**:

   o Some guests may have billing arrangements set up by a third party, such as a company, government agency, or travel agency. In such cases, billing instructions will specify what portion of the charges the third party will cover and which expenses the guest must pay personally.

6. **Traveler's Checks and Vouchers**:

   o Although less common today, some hotels still accept traveler's checks or hotel vouchers. These are more typical for international guests, especially in destinations frequented by tourists.

Providing diverse payment methods enhances convenience for guests and can increase satisfaction with the hotel's services.

Understanding Billing Instructions and Guest Folios

Guest folios and billing instructions are essential documents for recording, managing, and tracking guest expenses. Folios provide an itemized account of all charges incurred during a guest's stay, while billing instructions clarify how and by whom these charges will be settled.

1. **Billing Instructions**:

    o Billing instructions are often provided during booking and detail how the guest's expenses will be handled. For example, a company may cover lodging costs for a business traveler but require the guest to pay for incidentals.

    o Front desk staff must carefully review and input these instructions into the

Property Management System (PMS) to avoid billing errors and ensure accuracy at check-out.

2. **Guest Folios**:

o A guest folio is an electronic or printed account detailing every charge related to the guest's stay, including room rates, dining, taxes, service fees, and any incidentals. This folio is updated in real-time as charges are incurred.

o Front desk staff should review the folio periodically to ensure its accuracy, as this document serves as the official record for billing at check-out.

3. **Types of Folios**:

o **Individual Folios**: Track charges for individual guests or personal reservations.

- o **Master Folios**: Used for groups or corporate bookings, where multiple guests' expenses are managed under one main folio, often with separate breakdowns per guest or room.

- o **Split Folios**: Sometimes, guests request that specific charges be split between personal and company accounts. A split folio system allows front desk staff to categorize certain expenses (like room rate versus dining) to different folios or payers.

Understanding how to set up and maintain guest folios ensures accurate billing and helps avoid disputes at check-out.

Processing Payments and Managing Guest Accounts

Processing payments efficiently and managing guest accounts throughout their stay is crucial for an organized and error-free billing system.

1. **Pre-authorization at Check-In**:

   o Upon check-in, hotels generally pre-authorize the guest's credit card, which involves temporarily holding an amount on the card to cover potential charges. This practice prevents financial discrepancies and confirms that the guest has a means to cover their expenses.

   o Pre-authorizations typically include the room rate, taxes, and an additional amount for incidentals.

2. **Posting Charges to Guest Accounts**:

   o During the guest's stay, various charges (such as dining, room service, and laundry) are posted to their account or folio. Front desk staff and other departments must accurately and promptly post these charges to ensure the folio reflects all expenses.

o Any packages, discounts, or complimentary services must be recorded correctly to avoid confusion at check-out.

3. **Finalizing Payment at Check-Out**:

o At check-out, the front office reconciles the guest's folio, ensuring all charges are accurate and up to date. The guest is then provided with a detailed breakdown of the charges, which they review and settle using their chosen payment method.

o Front desk staff should confirm any pending charges, answer questions, and address any concerns the guest might have before processing the final payment.

4. **Refunds and Adjustments**:

- o If errors or overcharges are identified, the front office may process refunds or adjustments. For example, if the guest was mistakenly charged for an amenity they did not use, the charge should be removed promptly.

- o Refunds should be handled according to the hotel's policy, typically processed back to the original payment method.

Properly managing guest accounts ensures accurate billing and contributes to a positive guest experience.

Handling Disputes and Errors in Billing

Occasionally, guests may dispute charges or identify billing errors. Addressing these issues promptly and professionally is essential for maintaining guest satisfaction and avoiding negative reviews.

1. **Common Billing Disputes**:

    o Disputes often arise from unexpected charges, such as mini-bar fees, room service, or internet access. Guests may also dispute charges for services they believe were complimentary or promotional.

    o Overcharges or double-billing are other frequent sources of dispute and typically stem from system errors or miscommunication between departments.

2. **Best Practices for Resolving Disputes**:

    o **Listen and Acknowledge**: Begin by listening carefully to the guest's concerns. Acknowledge their frustration and express a willingness to investigate and resolve the issue.

- o **Review Folio Details**: Examine the guest's folio thoroughly and check for errors or discrepancies. Communicate with relevant departments if the dispute involves amenities or services beyond front desk operations.

- o **Offer Solutions**: If a genuine error occurred, offer an immediate adjustment or refund and apologize for the inconvenience. For charges that are valid but unexpected, explain the charges clearly and, if possible, offer a goodwill gesture (such as a small discount) to satisfy the guest.

3. **Preventing Billing Errors**:

- o Ensuring each department accurately records charges and follows proper protocols can prevent most billing errors. Regular audits and reviews of folios by the front office team further reduce the likelihood of mistakes.

o Staff should also be proactive in communicating with guests about potential charges, especially for additional services, ensuring transparency and avoiding surprises.

4. **Handling Escalated Billing Disputes**:

o If a guest remains dissatisfied with the resolution provided, the front office manager or a senior team member may step in to handle the situation. In cases where the dispute cannot be resolved on-site, hotels may offer to follow up after the guest's departure.

Resolving billing disputes with patience, empathy, and clear communication helps maintain a positive guest relationship, even in challenging situations.

Managing billing and payment procedures accurately is essential for the smooth operation of the front office and contributes significantly to guest satisfaction. By understanding payment methods, maintaining accurate guest folios, processing payments efficiently, and handling disputes professionally, the front office ensures a transparent and satisfying financial experience for guests.

Chapter 8: Check-out and Departure Process

The check-out and departure process are a critical stage in the guest journey, marking the final interaction between the guest and the hotel. A smooth, well-organized check-out experience leaves a lasting positive impression, which can influence guest satisfaction, reviews, and future loyalty. This chapter explores how to prepare for check-out, the step-by-step check-out process, handling feedback, and farewell etiquette, as well as follow-up actions to ensure a seamless guest experience.

Preparation for Guest Check-out

Preparation for guest check-out begins well before the guest reaches the front desk, involving several behind-the-scenes activities to ensure the process is smooth and efficient.

1. **Review Guest Folios**:

   o The front desk should review each departing guest's folio to ensure all charges are accurate and up to date. This includes room charges, dining expenses, mini-bar items, and any additional services like spa or laundry.

   o By reviewing the folio ahead of time, the staff can identify any potential discrepancies and address them proactively to avoid delays at check-out.

2. **Verify Billing Instructions**:

   o Confirm that billing instructions are in line with the guest's or company's preferences, especially for group or corporate bookings. This may include splitting charges between personal and company expenses or ensuring that specific charges are covered by third-party payers.

3. **Check for Pre-Departure Requests**:

   o Some guests may have made specific requests related to their departure, such as arranging airport transfers, printing boarding passes, or extending check-out time. Ensuring these requests are handled in advance contributes to a smooth check-out experience.

   o Special requests, such as luggage assistance or in-room check-out, should also be documented and communicated with relevant departments.

4. **Prepare Invoices and Documentation**:

o For business travelers or guests requiring itemized receipts, preparing invoices in advance helps expedite the check-out process. The invoices should include all relevant charges, including room rates, taxes, and any additional expenses.

Being well-prepared allows the front office team to efficiently handle guest departures and provide a positive final experience.

Steps in the Check-out Process

The check-out process involves several key steps, including settling accounts, issuing invoices, and processing payments.

1. **Welcoming the Guest for Check-out**:

   o Greet the departing guest warmly and confirm that they are ready to check out. A friendly and courteous approach helps set a positive tone for the interaction, creating a professional and respectful atmosphere.

2. Reviewing the Folio with the Guest:

- o Present the folio to the guest, giving them a chance to review all charges before payment. This step is crucial in ensuring that the guest is comfortable with the charges and has an opportunity to clarify any discrepancies.

- o Offer a printed or digital copy of the folio if the guest prefers to keep a record of their stay.

3. Settling Accounts:

- o Ask the guest to confirm their preferred payment method, whether it's a credit card, mobile payment, or another option. If the guest has pre-authorized a card, confirm that they are comfortable finalizing the payment on that card.

o Process the payment securely and provide a receipt. If the guest has any outstanding charges, ensure these are settled before finalizing the account.

4. **Issuing Invoices and Finalizing Documentation**:

    o After payment is processed, provide the guest with a finalized invoice detailing their charges. For corporate guests or those on business trips, this documentation may be essential for expense reporting.

    o For group bookings, guests may need separate invoices or detailed summaries, which should be prepared according to the group's requirements.

5. **Releasing Pre-Authorizations**:

    o After settling the account, release any pre-authorized holds on the guest's credit card. Releasing these funds is essential to ensure guests do not experience unnecessary holds on their credit.

An efficient check-out process demonstrates the hotel's attention to detail and respect for the guest's time, contributing to a positive final impression.

Handling Feedback During Check-out

Check-out is an excellent opportunity to gather feedback from guests about their stay, providing insights that can help improve service quality.

1. **Inviting Feedback**:

   o Politely ask guests if they would like to share feedback about their stay. This can be done in a conversational tone or through a short survey provided at check-out.

o For guests who seem hesitant, offer an easy way to leave feedback later, such as an email link or online survey, allowing them to share their thoughts in their own time.

2. **Listening to Compliments and Complaints**:

o If a guest shares positive feedback, acknowledge it with gratitude and let them know you're happy they enjoyed their stay. Positive feedback boosts morale and reinforces quality service standards.

o For complaints, listen attentively without interrupting. Thank the guest for bringing their concern to your attention and offer a brief apology if appropriate. For unresolved issues, reassure the guest that their feedback will be reviewed by management.

3. **Noting Feedback for Improvement**:

- o Front desk staff should document all feedback, especially recurring issues or suggestions, and share it with management. Constructive feedback is valuable for identifying areas of improvement and implementing service enhancements.

4. **Responding to Reviews and Ratings**:

- o Some guests may mention that they plan to leave an online review. Encourage them to share their experience and assure them that their feedback is valued. Positive reviews contribute to the hotel's reputation, while negative reviews provide insights into potential improvements.

By creating an open, welcoming environment for feedback, the front office staff demonstrates the hotel's commitment to continuous improvement.

Farewell Etiquette and Follow-up Actions

The farewell and follow-up after a guest's departure can be just as impactful as any other stage in their stay. A warm and sincere farewell leaves a lasting positive impression and may encourage repeat business.

1. **Farewell Etiquette**:

    o Thank the guest sincerely for choosing to stay at the hotel, and wish them a pleasant journey. A farewell can include friendly parting phrases like, *"We hope to see you again,"* or *"Safe travels and thank you for staying with us."*

    o If possible, accompany guests to the door or arrange transportation, especially for VIPs or special guests. A personalized farewell gesture can leave a memorable impression.

2. **Offering Assistance with Departure**:

○ If the guest requires assistance with luggage or transportation, ensure the arrangements are managed smoothly. A bell attendant may escort the guest to their car, or a shuttle service may be arranged for airport transfers.

○ For guests with specific departure needs, such as arranging for secure storage of items or retrieving forgotten belongings, front office staff should handle these requests promptly.

3. **Follow-up Actions**:

○ **Post-Stay Emails**: Many hotels send a follow-up email after check-out, thanking the guest and inviting them to complete a post-stay survey or share their experience online. These emails reinforce positive memories and help the hotel gather feedback.

- ○ **Lost and Found**: If any items are left behind, notify the guest and arrange for them to retrieve the items or have them shipped. A quick response to lost and found issues demonstrates care and attention.

- ○ **Loyalty Program Invitations**: For frequent guests or new visitors, a follow-up email may include an invitation to join the hotel's loyalty program. This can encourage future stays and build long-term guest relationships.

4. **Recording Guest Preferences**:

- ○ The front office team should record any notable guest preferences, requests, or feedback in the hotel's Property Management System (PMS) for future reference. This information helps personalize future stays and improves service consistency.

A genuine farewell and attentive follow-up actions enhance the guest's overall experience and increase the likelihood of repeat visits.

By managing each step of the check-out and departure process with care, efficiency, and attention to detail, the front office team creates a positive final impression, fostering guest satisfaction, loyalty, and the likelihood of positive reviews. The farewell and follow-up actions are essential in reinforcing the hotel's commitment to excellent service and building lasting guest relationships.

Chapter 9: Telephone Etiquette and Call Management

Telephone etiquette is a crucial skill for front office staff in the hospitality industry. The telephone is often the first point of contact for guests, and the manner in which calls are handled can significantly impact the guest's perception of the hotel. This chapter focuses on the importance of professional telephone etiquette, handling guest calls, managing multiple calls, and techniques for dealing with difficult or challenging calls.

Importance of Professional Telephone Etiquette

The front office is the face of the hotel, and every interaction — including those over the phone — is an opportunity to make a positive impression. Professional telephone etiquette not only reflects the hotel's standards but also contributes to effective communication and guest satisfaction.

1. **First Impressions Matter**:

   o A guest's first interaction with the hotel, often via phone, sets the tone for their entire stay. A friendly, polite, and professional tone immediately reassures the guest that they are in good hands and will receive the level of service they expect.

o Missteps in telephone etiquette, such as speaking too casually, using inappropriate language, or failing to be attentive, can negatively affect the guest's perception of the hotel.

2. **Professionalism**:

   o Front office staff should maintain a calm, courteous, and patient demeanor at all times. A professional voice, even in stressful situations, helps convey competence and builds trust with the guest.

   o Avoiding slang, using proper grammar, and speaking clearly and confidently all contribute to a positive phone interaction.

3. **Clear Communication**:

   o Clear, concise communication is essential for effective call management.

The staff must be able to listen actively, take accurate messages, and convey information without causing confusion.

o By ensuring that guests' inquiries are answered comprehensively and professionally, the hotel enhances its reputation for high-quality customer service.

Handling Guest Calls, Inquiries, and Requests

Guests often use the telephone to inquire about hotel services, make reservations, or request assistance during their stay. Handling these calls with efficiency and accuracy is essential for ensuring guest satisfaction.

1. **Greeting the Guest**:

   o Always begin a call with a professional greeting. This typically includes the hotel's name, the department the guest is calling, and the staff member's name. For example, *"Good morning, thank you for calling [Hotel Name], this is [Your Name] at the front desk. How may I assist you today?"*

o The greeting should be warm and welcoming, setting a positive tone for the conversation.

2. **Listening and Understanding the Guest's Request:**

o Active listening is vital to understanding the guest's needs. Avoid interrupting the guest, and allow them to fully express their request or concern before responding.

o Paraphrase or repeat key information back to the guest to confirm understanding. For instance, *"Just to confirm, you would like to reserve a room for two nights with a king-sized bed, correct?"*

3. **Providing Accurate Information**:

   o Front office staff must be familiar with the hotel's services and facilities to provide accurate and up-to-date information. This includes details about room availability, hotel amenities, check-in/check-out times, and local attractions.

   o If the information is not readily available, inform the guest that you will find out and get back to them promptly. Avoid guessing or providing inaccurate details.

4. **Handling Special Requests**:

   o When a guest makes a special request, such as a room upgrade, extra amenities, or late check-out, staff must check availability and confirm that the request can be accommodated.

- ○ Special requests should be documented and communicated to the appropriate department, such as housekeeping, housekeeping, or the bell desk, to ensure fulfillment.

5. **Making Reservations**:

- ○ If the call is for a reservation, ensure all relevant details are captured, including guest names, dates, room types, special requirements, and payment information.

- ○ Send a confirmation to the guest once the reservation is made, and provide clear instructions regarding check-in procedures.

Managing Multiple Calls and Prioritizing Responses

Front office staff often handle several calls simultaneously, particularly during peak hours, which can be a challenging task. Effective call management and prioritization are essential to ensure each guest receives the attention they need without delay.

1. **Answering Calls Promptly**:

   o Always aim to answer calls within three rings, ensuring the guest feels attended to. Prolonged waiting times can frustrate guests and create a negative impression of the hotel.

   o If calls cannot be answered immediately, place the guest on a brief hold and check back frequently to update them on the situation.

2. **Prioritizing Calls**:

o In some cases, you may need to prioritize certain calls based on urgency or importance. For instance, a guest calling with a check-in inquiry or reservation issue should be given precedence over a general inquiry.

o For emergency calls or urgent situations (e.g., a guest reporting a safety concern), respond immediately and escalate the situation to the appropriate department if necessary.

3. **Managing Hold Times**:

o If it's necessary to place a caller on hold, inform the guest first, and ask for their permission. For example, *"May I place you on hold for a moment while I check that information?"*

o While the guest is on hold, avoid leaving them waiting for too long.

Check back with them every 30-60 seconds to confirm that they're still on hold and to apologize for any delay.

4. **Transferring Calls Effectively**:

   o If you need to transfer a call to another department, inform the guest beforehand, and ensure that the right person is available to take the call. Always introduce the guest to the next person to avoid making the transfer feel abrupt.

   o For example, *"I'll be transferring you to our concierge, who can assist you with local tours. Please hold for a moment."*

5. **Managing Call Volume**:

   o During busy times, such as peak check-in/check-out periods, managing call volume can be overwhelming. Efficient call routing, using a well-organized call queue, and keeping the phone system updated with out-of-office messages (if appropriate) can help streamline operations.

o Front office staff should remain calm and focused even during high-pressure moments to maintain professionalism.

Techniques for Handling Difficult Calls

Difficult or challenging calls can arise for many reasons, such as guest complaints, misunderstandings, or high expectations. It's important to handle these calls with care and professionalism to resolve the situation and maintain the guest's trust.

1. **Stay Calm and Composed**:

   o When handling difficult calls, always maintain a calm, steady, and professional demeanor, even if the guest is upset or frustrated. Avoid reacting emotionally or raising your voice.

○ Practice active listening and demonstrate empathy to acknowledge the guest's feelings, such as, *"I understand this situation is frustrating, and I apologize for the inconvenience."*

2. **Empathy and Apology**:

○ Show empathy by acknowledging the guest's concerns and apologizing for the inconvenience they've experienced. An apology can go a long way in diffusing tension and making the guest feel heard and valued.

○ Even if the hotel is not at fault, expressing regret for the guest's frustration can help calm the situation. For example, *"I'm sorry you've had this experience. Let's work together to resolve this as quickly as possible."*

3. **Remain Professional**:

   o Even when faced with an irate or rude guest, professionalism is key. Stay polite, avoid arguing, and refrain from using defensive language. If the situation becomes increasingly difficult, offer to transfer the call to a supervisor or manager who can provide further assistance.

   o For example, *"I understand you're upset. Let me transfer you to my manager, who will be able to assist you further."*

4. **Offering Solutions and Alternatives**:

   o Once the issue is understood, focus on finding a resolution. Offer solutions or alternatives whenever possible, and clearly explain the steps that will be taken to resolve the issue.

o If you cannot resolve the issue immediately, be transparent about the timeline and assure the guest that their concerns are being taken seriously. For example, *"I'm going to look into this right away and will update you shortly."*

5. **Ending the Call on a Positive Note**:

o After the issue is resolved, thank the guest for their patience and cooperation. Confirm that all their concerns have been addressed and that they feel satisfied with the solution.

o End the call by offering additional assistance, such as, *"Is there anything else I can assist you with today?"*

By maintaining professional telephone etiquette, efficiently managing guest calls, and using appropriate techniques for handling difficult situations, front office staff can enhance the guest experience, improve guest satisfaction, and maintain the hotel's reputation for high-quality service. Effective call management also ensures that operations run smoothly, even during busy times, and that all guests' needs are met promptly and professionally.

Chapter 10: Guest Relations and Handling Complaints

Guest relations is a core function of the front office, directly impacting guest satisfaction, loyalty, and overall experience at the hotel. How staff manage guest interactions, especially when problems arise, can determine whether a guest returns and whether they leave with a positive or negative impression of the hotel. This chapter focuses on the importance of guest relations, techniques for handling complaints, building rapport, and managing critical situations to recover guest satisfaction.

Importance of Guest Relations in Front Office Operations

Guest relations refers to the efforts and strategies used by front office staff to build and maintain positive relationships with hotel guests. These relationships are crucial for ensuring guest loyalty and creating memorable experiences that encourage repeat visits.

1. **First Point of Contact**:

    o The front office is often the first and last point of contact for guests, making it essential for the staff to make a lasting, positive impression. From the moment the guest arrives to their departure, how their needs are met and how their concerns are handled will define their overall satisfaction.

o Building strong guest relations means not only addressing immediate needs but also anticipating future ones, creating a seamless and personalized experience for each guest.

2. **Influence on Guest Satisfaction**:

o A key objective of guest relations is to enhance guest satisfaction, which has a direct impact on the hotel's reputation and bottom line. Satisfied guests are more likely to return, leave positive reviews, and recommend the hotel to others.

o Negative experiences, if not handled well, can lead to complaints, poor reviews, and a loss of business. A proactive, attentive approach to guest relations can prevent issues from escalating.

3. **Building Long-Term Relationships**:

- ○ Guest relations is about more than just one-time service it's about cultivating relationships that last. Loyal guests who feel valued and appreciated are more likely to return and form long-term connections with the hotel.

- ○ By keeping track of guest preferences, previous complaints, and special requests, the hotel can deliver a more personalized experience, which makes guests feel special and more likely to stay again.

Techniques for Handling Guest Complaints and Issues

Even with excellent service, issues and complaints are inevitable. How they are addressed is a key factor in determining guest satisfaction and future loyalty. The goal is not only to resolve the issue but also to do so in a way that strengthens the relationship with the guest.

1. **Listen Actively and Empathetically**:

   o The first step in handling a complaint is to listen carefully to the guest's concerns. Do not interrupt the guest as they describe the problem. Give them the opportunity to express their feelings and frustrations.

   o Show empathy by acknowledging their feelings. For example, *"I can understand how frustrating this must be for you. I'm really sorry you had to experience that."* This validates the guest's feelings and helps to build rapport.

2. **Stay Calm and Professional**:

   o Even if the guest is upset or angry, it's essential for the staff to remain calm, composed, and professional. A cool-headed, respectful demeanor helps defuse tension and maintains the guest's confidence in the front office's ability to handle the situation.

o Avoid becoming defensive or arguing with the guest. Instead, focus on understanding the issue and working towards a solution.

3. **Apologize and Take Responsibility**:

o Offer a sincere apology, regardless of whether the hotel is at fault. An apology demonstrates care and concern and shows the guest that their issue is being taken seriously.

o For example, *"I apologize for the inconvenience this has caused you. Let me see how we can resolve this for you."* This simple phrase can go a long way in calming down a dissatisfied guest.

4. **Investigate and Assess the Situation**:

   o After acknowledging the complaint, investigate the issue. This may involve checking records, speaking with other staff members, or assessing the situation firsthand.

   o It's important to gather all the facts before proposing a solution to ensure that the guest's complaint is fully understood.

5. **Propose a Solution or Alternative**:

   o Once the situation is assessed, offer a solution or alternative that satisfies the guest. This could involve offering a room change, a discount, a complimentary service, or an expedited resolution to the issue at hand.

o Be clear and transparent about what you can and cannot offer. If the issue cannot be immediately resolved, communicate the steps you will take to fix it and keep the guest informed of the progress.

6. **Follow Up**:

o After resolving the complaint, follow up with the guest to ensure they are satisfied with the outcome. A simple phone call or email a few hours or a day later can reinforce the hotel's commitment to guest satisfaction.

o For example, *"I just wanted to check in and ensure everything is to your liking now that your issue has been addressed. Please let us know if there's anything else we can do for you."*

Building Rapport and Maintaining Guest Satisfaction

Strong guest relations are based on creating an ongoing connection with guests, making them feel valued, and ensuring they are satisfied with every aspect of their stay.

1. **Personalization**:

   ○ Remembering guests' names, preferences, and previous interactions is essential for building rapport. Personalization can be as simple as remembering a guest's favorite room type, a dietary restriction, or their preference for a particular type of pillow.

   ○ Use guest history to make recommendations or offer tailored services that will enhance their stay. This creates a sense of recognition and shows that the hotel cares about their individual needs.

2. **Anticipating Guest Needs**:

- o Anticipating a guest's needs before they ask is one of the most effective ways to maintain satisfaction. This could involve ensuring that a guest has everything they need for their stay, such as extra towels, a newspaper in the morning, or local recommendations.

- o Offering thoughtful touches like a welcome note, a birthday greeting, or a surprise upgrade can make a guest feel special and appreciated.

3. **Consistency**:

- o Consistency in service is key to maintaining guest satisfaction. Front office staff must ensure that the level of service provided to each guest is consistently high, regardless of the guest's status or length of stay.

o This means maintaining a professional demeanor, being courteous, and following through on commitments, whether the guest is a VIP or a first-time visitor.

4. **Show Appreciation**:

o Show appreciation for guests who return to the hotel, as well as those who provide positive feedback. A simple thank-you note or a gesture of appreciation, such as a complimentary drink or small gift, can go a long way in building loyalty.

o Recognizing repeat guests and offering them loyalty benefits fosters a deeper connection and encourages them to return.

Handling Critical Situations and Guest Recovery Techniques

In some cases, guest complaints or issues may escalate into critical situations that require immediate attention and intervention. These situations could involve safety concerns, billing disputes, or situations where a guest feels their needs are not being met.

1. **Remain Calm Under Pressure**:

   o In critical situations, remaining calm is essential for resolving the issue effectively. A panic-stricken response can escalate the situation, so it is vital to stay composed, even in stressful circumstances.

   o Take a deep breath, assess the situation logically, and prioritize finding a solution.

2. **Escalate When Necessary**:

   o If the situation is beyond the front office team's ability to resolve, escalate it to a manager or senior staff member.

This ensures that the guest's concerns are addressed at a higher level, and it can help de-escalate the situation.

o For example, *"I understand that this is a serious concern. I am going to have my manager speak with you directly to ensure this is handled properly."*

3. **Guest Recovery and Compensation**:

o In cases where the hotel has failed to meet a guest's expectations, offering compensation can help turn a negative experience into a positive one. This could include offering a discount, a free service, or a complimentary night's stay.

o Recovery efforts should be sincere and focus on making things right. It's important to convey to the guest that the hotel values their feedback and is committed to resolving the issue.

4. **Follow Through and Prevent Future Issues**:

  o After a critical situation has been resolved, ensure that the issue does not recur by following up with the guest and reviewing internal processes to identify improvements.

  o For example, if a guest experienced issues with cleanliness, investigate the root cause and improve training or housekeeping procedures to prevent the same issue from happening again.

By handling guest complaints effectively and focusing on building strong relationships, the front office can ensure that guests leave with a positive impression, even if issues arise during their stay. Good guest relations foster loyalty, encourage repeat business, and strengthen the hotel's reputation for excellent service. Whether dealing with minor concerns or critical issues, the ability to recover a guest's satisfaction is an essential skill for the front office team.

Chapter 11: Night Audit Procedures

The night audit is a critical process in hotel operations, ensuring that all financial transactions for the day are accurate and accounted for, and preparing the hotel's system for the next day. This chapter delves into the purpose of the night audit, the steps involved, the generation of daily reports, and how to identify and correct any errors in transactions.

Purpose of the Night Audit and Daily Closure Process

The night audit serves several key functions in hotel operations, ensuring that financial and operational data is up to date, reconciled, and ready for the next day's operations.

1. **Financial Reconciliation**:

   o The primary purpose of the night audit is to verify and reconcile all financial transactions that have taken place during the day. This includes payments for rooms, food and beverage charges, miscellaneous services, and other guest expenses. The goal is to ensure that the hotel's books are accurate and that all transactions are correctly posted to the appropriate accounts.

   o It also involves reconciling the cash drawer and credit card transactions to ensure that all payments are correctly processed.

2. **Daily Closure and System Reset**:

   o The night audit process includes closing out the current day's transactions and resetting the system for the following day. This prepares the property management system (PMS) to start fresh, ensuring that the hotel's records are accurate for the next day's operations.

○ For example, it involves closing the guest folios (accounts), posting charges to the general ledger, and updating room availability for the next day.

3. **Ensuring Accurate Data for Reporting**:

○ The audit provides accurate, up-to-date information for various reports that will be used by management to assess the hotel's financial and operational performance. These reports help management make decisions regarding revenue management, marketing strategies, and operational improvements.

- Reports such as room occupancy, revenue per available room (RevPAR), and daily financial summaries are generated during the night audit process.

4. **Security and Fraud Prevention**:

- The night audit also acts as a security checkpoint to ensure that all transactions are legitimate. Any discrepancies or unusual activity in guest accounts can be flagged and investigated.

- This process also ensures that all payments made throughout the day have been processed, preventing any discrepancies in the financial records.

Steps Involved in the Night Audit Process

The night audit process involves a series of steps, typically performed at the end of the business day, to ensure the hotel's financial systems are balanced and updated.

1. **Verify and Post All Transactions**:

    o All charges and payments from the day must be reviewed and posted to the correct guest accounts. This includes charges for rooms, food and beverages, spa treatments, telephone calls, and any other incidentals.

    o Post any charges that were not yet processed during the day and ensure that credit card payments, cash transactions, and other forms of payment are recorded.

2. **Check for Unsettled Folios**:

    o Identify any guest folios that are not yet settled or have outstanding balances. This can include checking for guests who have not completed check-out or those with unpaid bills.

o For unsettled folios, follow up with the appropriate department (such as the front desk or accounting) to settle the bill or investigate why it has not been closed.

3. **Reconcile Cash and Credit Transactions**:

o Reconcile all cash and credit card transactions to ensure that the amounts received match the payments posted in the system. This includes checking the cash drawer for any discrepancies, reconciling the receipts, and ensuring credit card transactions have been successfully processed.

o If there are discrepancies, they must be identified and corrected before proceeding further with the night audit.

4. **Close Guest Accounts and Post Room Revenue**:

   o Close out all guest accounts, ensuring that all charges for room stays, incidentals, and taxes have been posted correctly. Room revenue is then transferred to the hotel's general ledger.

   o This step is important for generating accurate daily revenue reports and for tax purposes.

5. **Recalculate Room Availability**:

   o Update room availability in the system for the next day's check-ins and check-outs. This helps to ensure that the property management system accurately reflects the availability of rooms for reservations.

o If necessary, reassign rooms based on availability and adjust for no-shows or last-minute cancellations.

6. **Generate Reports**:

o Generate key daily reports, including:

- **Revenue Reports**: Detailing the total revenue for the day, including room revenue, food and beverage revenue, and other sources of income.

- **Occupancy Reports**: Analyzing the hotel's occupancy levels, including room availability, sold rooms, and the occupancy percentage.

- **Guest Activity Reports**: Summarizing guest check-ins, check-outs, arrivals, and departures.

- **Payment Reports**: Detailing payments received from guests, including cash, credit cards, and other forms of payment.

- **Miscellaneous Reports**: Any other specific reports required for internal management or departmental use.

7. **Post Daily Transactions to the General Ledger**:

   o After reconciling all transactions and generating reports, post all day's financial data to the general ledger for accounting purposes.

   o This ensures that all financial transactions are recorded in the hotel's accounting system, preparing the hotel's accounts for external audits and tax reporting.

8. Finalize and Reset the System:

- After completing the audit and ensuring everything is balanced, finalize the night audit process by resetting the hotel's property management system (PMS) for the next day.

- This includes setting the date to the following day, updating room availability, and resetting operational parameters.

9. Complete the Shift Handover:

- Once the night audit is complete, the night auditor should prepare for a handover to the day shift. This includes reviewing reports, noting any issues or discrepancies, and ensuring that the next shift is informed of any critical information regarding guest arrivals, departures, or operational updates.

Generating Daily Reports and Analyzing Room Occupancy

Generating accurate daily reports is one of the key responsibilities of the night audit. These reports provide vital information for hotel management and help assess both the hotel's operational and financial performance.

1. **Revenue Reports**:

    o These reports provide a detailed breakdown of the total revenue generated from all departments in the hotel. This includes room revenue, food and beverage sales, spa services, and other ancillary services.

    o Revenue reports can be further analyzed by different departments to assess performance, identify trends, and make adjustments to pricing strategies.

2. Occupancy Reports:

- o Occupancy reports are essential for analyzing room usage and efficiency. These reports provide details on the number of rooms sold, the total number of rooms available, and the occupancy rate.

- o Analyzing these reports helps management understand demand patterns, which can assist in pricing decisions and inventory management.

3. Room Revenue and Average Daily Rate (ADR):

- o The average daily rate (ADR) is a key performance indicator (KPI) for hotel performance. It's calculated by dividing total room revenue by the number of rooms sold. The night audit process allows management to monitor

142

ADR and compare it to previous periods or industry standards.

o Room revenue is calculated by multiplying the number of rooms sold by the room rate, helping to assess the hotel's performance and track revenue goals.

Identifying and Correcting Errors in Transactions

During the night audit, errors in transactions are often identified. These can include billing mistakes, unposted charges, or incorrect payments. Correcting these errors is crucial for maintaining financial accuracy and guest satisfaction.

1. **Identifying Common Errors**:

    o **Unposted Charges**: Charges such as room service, minibar items, or spa services may not have been posted to the guest's account. The night auditor must verify that all charges are accurately recorded.

- o **Billing Errors**: Guests may have been charged incorrectly for room rates, upgrades, or taxes. It is important to identify these errors before finalizing the guest's account.

- o **Duplicate Transactions**: A guest may have been charged multiple times for the same service or item. This can be caused by system errors or manual mistakes.

2. **Correcting Errors**:

- o Once an error is identified, the night auditor must take corrective action by reversing the incorrect charge and posting the correct transaction. This may require issuing refunds, adjustments to room rates, or crediting the guest's folio.

144

o If the error is identified after the guest has checked out, the auditor should process the necessary adjustments to the guest's account and ensure that the credit or charge is reflected in the hotel's system.

3. **Documenting Adjustments**:

o All corrections should be documented thoroughly. This includes noting the reason for the correction, the amount, and any supporting details, such as a guest complaint or a system error.

o Proper documentation helps maintain transparency and ensures that all adjustments are legitimate and properly accounted for.

The night audit is essential for ensuring that the hotel's financial systems are accurate, up-to-date, and ready for the next day's operations. By performing a detailed review of all transactions, generating key reports, and identifying errors, the night auditor plays a vital role in maintaining financial accuracy and preparing for the next day's operations. This process contributes to the overall efficiency and profitability of the hotel.

Chapter 12: Safety and Security in Front Office Operations

Safety and security are paramount in the hospitality industry, especially within the front office department, as it is often the first point of contact for guests when emergencies arise. The front office plays a crucial role in maintaining a safe environment for both guests and staff while ensuring that safety protocols are followed correctly during routine operations and in the event of an emergency. This chapter covers the key aspects of safety and security in front office operations, including guest safety, hotel security protocols, handling lost and found items, emergency procedures, and collaborating with security staff.

Understanding Guest Safety and Hotel Security Protocols

1. **Guest Safety: A Top Priority**:

   o Ensuring the safety of guests is one of the most important responsibilities of the front office. The front desk staff are responsible for creating a secure environment by implementing security measures and responding promptly to any safety concerns.

   o Guest safety includes physical security, such as protecting guests from theft or harm, as well as emotional security, like making guests feel welcome and assured that their well-being is a top concern.

2. **Hotel Security Protocols**:

   o Hotels typically have strict security protocols in place to protect both guests and property. Front office staff must be familiar with these protocols and follow them consistently. These protocols can include access control systems (key cards, locks), surveillance cameras, alarm systems, and secure handling of guest information.

o Front desk personnel are also responsible for verifying the identity of guests upon check-in, ensuring that only authorized individuals gain access to rooms and facilities. This is especially important for rooms with high-profile guests or sensitive information.

3. **Key Security**:

o Proper handling of room keys or key cards is critical for guest safety. Front office staff must ensure that keys are not misplaced or given to the wrong person. This includes keeping track of who receives which key and ensuring that guests understand how to safely store and return their keys.

4. **Confidentiality of Guest Information**:

o Safeguarding guest information, including personal details and payment data, is a key component of hotel security. Front office staff must follow privacy laws and hotel policies to protect sensitive guest data from unauthorized access or breaches.

o This includes adhering to secure data storage practices, ensuring that computers and systems are password protected, and properly disposing of any documents with guest information.

Handling Lost and Found Items

1. **Importance of Proper Lost and Found Procedures**:

o Lost and found procedures are an important part of maintaining guest trust and satisfaction. Front office staff must handle lost and found items carefully, ensuring that they are securely stored and returned to the rightful owner.

o Guests may misplace personal belongings such as electronics, clothing, jewelry, or documents. Properly handling these items can enhance the guest experience and demonstrate the hotel's commitment to service.

2. **Logging Lost and Found Items**:

o The first step in handling lost and found items is documenting the item in a detailed log. This should include a description of the item, the date it was found, and where it was discovered. The log should also note any specific details that may help identify the item (e.g., serial numbers, distinguishing features).

o Staff must ensure that lost items are stored securely and that access to the storage area is restricted to authorized personnel only.

3. **Returning Lost Items to Guests**:

o When a guest inquiries about a lost item, front desk staff should first verify the guest's identity and confirm the details of the item. Once confirmed, the item should be returned promptly and in a secure manner.

o If the item cannot be returned in person (e.g., the guest has checked out), the hotel should arrange for secure shipping and provide the guest with tracking information.

4. Dealing with Unclaimed Items:

- o Unclaimed items should be handled according to hotel policy. This often includes storing items for a specified period (e.g., 30 days) and, after this time, donating, discarding, or auctioning unclaimed items.

- o A clear policy regarding lost and found items should be communicated to guests and staff to ensure consistency.

Procedures for Emergency Situations (Fire, Medical, Evacuation)

1. Fire Emergencies:

- o Fire safety is a critical concern for all hotels. Front office staff must be well-trained in fire safety procedures, including how to evacuate guests, alert emergency services, and ensure that the hotel's fire alarm system is working properly.

○ In the event of a fire, front desk staff should remain calm and immediately initiate the hotel's fire evacuation plan. This includes informing guests of the situation and directing them to safe evacuation routes.

○ Regular fire drills should be conducted to ensure that both staff and guests are familiar with fire safety procedures.

2. **Medical Emergencies**:

○ Front office staff should be trained to respond effectively in medical emergencies, whether it's assisting with a guest who is feeling unwell or coordinating with medical professionals in the event of a more serious situation.

○ Staff should know the location of the nearest medical facility or hospital and be able to assist guests in arranging transportation if needed. In some cases, hotels may have arrangements with local doctors or emergency medical services for immediate assistance.

o Front office staff should be familiar with basic first aid and CPR procedures and have access to first aid kits in case of emergencies.

3. **Evacuation Procedures**:

o In the event of an evacuation (such as for a fire, natural disaster, or other emergency), the front office must coordinate with security, emergency services, and other hotel departments to ensure guests are evacuated safely and efficiently.

o The front desk should have an evacuation plan that includes procedures for evacuating guests, informing them of the situation, and directing them to safe assembly areas. The hotel should also have designated evacuation routes, backup power systems, and trained staff to assist guests with mobility impairments.

4. **Crisis Communication**:

   o During an emergency, clear and calm communication is essential. Front office staff should provide guests with accurate and timely information and ensure that they remain informed throughout the event.

   o Communication should be handled in a manner that reduces panic, with staff directing guests to designated safe zones and offering assistance as needed.

Working with Security Staff and Protocols for Suspicious Activities

1. Collaboration with Security Staff:

- The front office team often works closely with hotel security to monitor and manage the safety of both guests and staff. Security staff are typically responsible for monitoring surveillance cameras, patrolling hotel grounds, and responding to suspicious activities or emergencies.

- Front office staff should be in regular communication with security personnel, providing them with any information related to security risks or unusual guest behavior. This collaboration ensures a prompt and efficient response to any safety concerns.

2. Protocols for Suspicious Activities:

o Front office staff must be trained to identify and report suspicious activities or individuals. This could include guests acting suspiciously, people attempting to gain unauthorized access to rooms, or unusual behavior that may indicate a security threat.

o Suspicious activities should be reported immediately to security or management. Front office staff should avoid confrontation with suspicious individuals and instead focus on gathering information discreetly and ensuring that security is notified promptly.

3. **Handling Threatening or Violent Guests**:

o If a guest becomes violent or threatening, front office staff should follow hotel protocol for managing such situations. This may involve involving   security   personnel, contacting law enforcement, or de-escalating the situation if possible.

o   In these instances, maintaining a calm and professional demeanor is critical to prevent escalation. Front office staff should avoid taking matters into their own hands and should instead focus on alerting appropriate authorities.

4. **Implementing   Emergency   Lockdown Procedures**:

o   In certain situations, such as a threat to guest safety, the hotel may need to initiate an emergency lockdown to secure all entrances and prevent unauthorized access.

o   Front office staff must be familiar with lockdown   procedures,   including notifying guests about the situation, securing   the   property,   and communicating with security and law enforcement.

Safety and security in front office operations are vital to creating a safe and comfortable environment for both guests and staff. From handling emergency situations like fires or medical emergencies to collaborating with security staff and ensuring the safe return of lost items, front office personnel play an essential role in maintaining the integrity of the hotel's operations. By adhering to established protocols, remaining vigilant, and responding swiftly to any potential threats, front office staff contribute to the overall safety and security of the hotel, enhancing guest satisfaction and ensuring the hotel's reputation as a safe, secure, and welcoming place.

Chapter 13: Role of Technology in Front Office

Technology plays a pivotal role in the front office of a hotel, enabling greater efficiency, enhancing guest experience, and optimizing operations. The integration of advanced systems and tools ensures smoother communication, streamlined processes, and improved service delivery. This chapter explores the essential role of technology in the front office, from Property Management Systems (PMS) to emerging trends like AI and chatbots, and how these technologies contribute to operational success and guest satisfaction.

Introduction to Property Management Systems (PMS)

1. **What is a Property Management System (PMS)?**

   A Property Management System (PMS) is a software application used by hotels to manage day-to-day operations such as reservations, guest check-ins/check-outs, room assignments, billing, and housekeeping coordination. It serves as the central hub for all guest information and hotel activities, ensuring data is integrated across all departments.

- o **Centralized Database**: A PMS centralizes guest and operational data, ensuring that all hotel departments are working with the same real-time information. This improves communication, reduces errors, and provides staff with the tools to deliver a seamless guest experience.

- o **Reservations Management**: The PMS allows front office staff to manage individual, group, and corporate reservations efficiently. It provides real-time availability, tracks bookings, and manages cancellations and modifications, ensuring that the hotel remains fully optimized.

- **Guest Profiles**: The PMS stores detailed guest information such as personal preferences, payment details, special requests, and previous stays, allowing for personalized services that enhance guest satisfaction.

- **Billing and Payment**: PMS handles all billing activities, including posting charges (room, F&B, etc.), generating invoices, and processing payments. It also assists in managing guest folios, providing a clear overview of each guest's account.

2. **Key Benefits of a PMS**:

  - **Efficiency and Automation**: Automating administrative tasks such as reservations, check-ins, and check-outs reduces manual errors and frees up staff to focus on guest interactions.

- o **Data Integration**: PMS systems integrate with other hotel software systems (such as POS systems, booking engines, and housekeeping management tools), allowing for more efficient operations and real-time data sharing.

- o **Revenue Management**: Many PMS systems include revenue management tools that help optimize room rates and availability, helping to increase occupancy and revenue.

Utilizing Front Office Software for Efficiency

1. **Front Office Software Functions**:

   - o **Check-in and Check-out Process**: Front office software automates the check-in and check-out process, allowing for quicker guest processing. Guests can be checked in using tablets or desktop terminals, with key cards being automatically issued.

- o **Room Assignments and Upgrades**: The system can match guests to rooms based on their preferences or the availability of upgraded rooms. Staff can also manage upgrades and room changes efficiently using the software.

- o **Guest Messaging and Communication**: Many front office software solutions now include communication tools for direct messaging with guests. This allows for personalized communication, such as pre-arrival information, room service requests, or addressing guest inquiries.

- o **Housekeeping Coordination**: Integration between front office software and housekeeping systems ensures that room statuses (clean, dirty, occupied) are updated in real time. This coordination optimizes room turnover and improves guest satisfaction.

2. **Enhancing Operational Efficiency**:

   o **Real-Time Updates**: Front office software provides real-time updates for reservations, guest profiles, billing information, and occupancy rates, allowing front desk agents to make informed decisions and respond promptly to guest needs.

   o **Centralized Communication**: With integrated messaging and alert systems, front desk staff can communicate directly with housekeeping, maintenance, and other departments to address guest needs and resolve issues without delays.

3. **Reporting and Analytics**:

o Front office software generates key reports on occupancy rates, revenue, guest demographics, and operational performance. This data is vital for managers to assess the hotel's performance and make informed business decisions.

o Revenue reports and financial summaries also help identify trends, manage costs, and ensure accurate billing.

Role of Mobile Apps and Self-Service Kiosks

1. **Mobile Apps**:

   o **Guest Interaction and Convenience**: Mobile apps are increasingly used to enhance guest engagement and improve convenience. Guests can check in/out, make special requests, and communicate with the front desk, all through their smartphones.

- **Room Control and Personalization**: Many hotel apps allow guests to control aspects of their room environment (such as lighting, temperature, and entertainment) via their mobile device, offering a personalized and more comfortable experience.

- **Mobile Key**: One of the most notable features of hotel mobile apps is the mobile key. Guests can bypass the front desk entirely and use their smartphones to unlock their room, reducing wait times and enhancing convenience.

- **Guest Loyalty and Marketing**: Mobile apps can also be used for loyalty programs, promotions, and offers, encouraging repeat bookings and fostering a sense of exclusivity and engagement with the brand.

2. **Self-Service Kiosks**:

   o **Self-Check-In/Check-Out**: Self-service kiosks allow guests to check in and check out without having to interact with the front desk staff, which speeds up the process, especially for guests arriving during peak hours. Kiosks can also allow guests to select their room preferences and print room keys.

   o **Payment and Billing**: Kiosks can process payments directly, allowing guests to settle their bills, view their charges, and receive an invoice. This reduces wait times and operational workload on the front desk.

   o **Guest Information and Requests**: Guests can use kiosks to request additional services (e.g., room service, wake-up calls) or obtain information about hotel amenities and local attractions. This enhances guest experience by providing them with more control over their stay.

Emerging Trends in Front Office Technology (AI, Chatbots)

1. **Artificial Intelligence (AI) in Front Office Operations**:

   o **AI-Powered Chatbots**: Chatbots are becoming more common in front office operations, providing instant assistance to guests via messaging platforms, mobile apps, or the hotel's website. Chatbots can handle a range of tasks, from answering frequently asked questions (FAQs) to managing simple requests like booking reservations, ordering room service, or providing local recommendations.

o **Personalization Through AI**: AI allows for advanced personalization, analyzing guest data and preferences to offer customized recommendations or anticipate guest needs before they are even expressed. For example, AI can suggest room upgrades, personalized amenities, or special packages based on a guest's profile.

o **Voice Assistants**: Voice recognition technology, integrated with in-room systems or mobile apps, enables guests to make requests simply by speaking. This can include adjusting room settings (e.g., lighting, temperature), ordering services, or requesting information about the hotel.

2. **Robotics and Automation**:

- o **Automated Check-In/Check-Out**: Some hotels are incorporating robotic check-in kiosks and self-service machines that allow guests to bypass the front desk altogether. This can lead to a faster, more efficient guest experience, particularly during high-traffic periods.

- o **Robot Concierge and Delivery**: Hotels are increasingly deploying robots for concierge duties, such as delivering amenities or providing basic information. These robots are a novel guest experience feature and can also be used for routine tasks like delivering towels or toiletries to rooms.

3. **Blockchain for Payment Security**:

- o Blockchain technology, known for its secure and transparent nature, is gaining traction in the hospitality industry for managing payments, loyalty programs, and reservations. It allows for faster, more secure transactions and could revolutionize the way hotel payments and guest data are handled.

4. **Data Analytics and Predictive Technology**:

   o Advanced data analytics is helping hotels forecast guest behavior, occupancy, and revenue more accurately. Predictive technology can be used for dynamic pricing, anticipating demand, and optimizing room allocation to maximize revenue.

   o Hotels are increasingly using data analytics to identify patterns in guest preferences and behavior, allowing for more targeted marketing and improved guest personalization.

Technology is transforming the way front office operations are conducted in the hotel industry, enhancing efficiency, personalization, and overall guest satisfaction. From Property Management Systems (PMS) to the use of mobile apps, self-service kiosks, and AI, technology is enabling front desk staff to streamline processes and deliver better service. Emerging trends like AI, robotics, and blockchain are set to further revolutionize the industry, making it easier for hotels to meet the evolving expectations of today's tech-savvy guests. As these technologies continue to evolve, the front office will play an increasingly vital role in shaping the guest experience and driving operational success.

Chapter 14: Managing Front Office Staff

Effective management of front office staff is critical to ensuring smooth operations and delivering exceptional guest service. The front office is the face of the hotel, and the behavior, skills, and efficiency of the team directly impact the guest experience. This chapter explores the essential aspects of managing front office staff, including recruitment, training, team development, scheduling, and fostering teamwork and leadership within the department.

Recruitment and Training of Front Office Staff

1. **Recruitment Process**:

   o **Identifying the Right Candidates**: The recruitment process for front office staff requires identifying candidates with the right skill set, personality, and passion for hospitality. Essential qualities include strong communication skills, customer service orientation, attention to detail, and the ability to work under pressure.

   o **Job Descriptions and Roles**: Clear and comprehensive job descriptions should outline the roles and responsibilities of front office staff, which may include tasks such as guest check-in/check-out, handling reservations, managing guest inquiries, and coordinating with other departments. These descriptions should also include the required qualifications, such as a background in hospitality or customer service.

o **Interviewing and Selection**: The interview process should assess both technical skills (e.g., knowledge of Property Management Systems, language proficiency) and soft skills (e.g., interpersonal communication, problem-solving ability). Role-playing exercises or situational questions can help evaluate a candidate's ability to handle typical front office scenarios.

o **Cultural Fit**: It is important to ensure that candidates align with the hotel's culture and values. Front office staff are often the first point of contact for guests, so their demeanor, professionalism, and personality should reflect the hotel's ethos.

2. **Training of Front Office Staff**:

o **Onboarding and Orientation**: A structured onboarding process ensures that new front office employees are familiar with the hotel's policies, procedures, and expectations. They should receive training on using the Property Management System (PMS), handling guest check-ins/check-outs, and understanding safety protocols.

o **Skill Development**: Regular training sessions are essential for developing staff's technical and interpersonal skills. This includes in-depth training on front office software, guest service techniques, communication skills, handling complaints, and emergency procedures.

o **Product Knowledge**: Front office staff should be well-versed in the hotel's facilities, services, and local attractions. This enables them to offer guests personalized recommendations and assist them effectively with any inquiries.

o **Cross-Training**: Cross-training staff in other departments, such as housekeeping, food and beverage, or concierge, enhances flexibility and helps staff understand the interconnectivity of hotel operations. This broadens their skill set and fosters better collaboration between departments.

Developing a Customer-Focused Team

1. Creating a Customer-Centric Culture:

- **Guest Satisfaction as a Priority**: Front office staff must be trained to prioritize guest satisfaction in all interactions. The emphasis should be on creating a positive, personalized experience for every guest, anticipating needs, and going above and beyond to exceed expectations.

- **Empowerment and Problem Solving**: Staff should be empowered to resolve guest issues promptly and efficiently, with a strong focus on finding solutions rather than just identifying problems. This fosters a sense of ownership and confidence among the team.

- **Feedback and Continuous Improvement**: A customer-focused team should value feedback both positive and negative as an opportunity for growth. Regularly soliciting guest feedback and using it to improve service delivery is essential for continuous improvement.

2. **Building Team Morale**:

   o **Recognition and Reward**: Recognizing and rewarding exceptional performance boosts morale and encourages staff to deliver their best work. Front office staff who feel appreciated are more likely to go the extra mile for guests.

   o **Motivational Activities**: Organizing team-building events, social activities, or friendly competitions can enhance camaraderie among front office staff. This fosters a positive work environment where employees feel engaged and motivated to provide excellent service.

3. **Setting Standards and Expectations**:

- ○ **Clear Expectations**: Setting clear, achievable goals and expectations for staff performance ensures that everyone is aligned and knows what is expected of them. This could include key performance indicators (KPIs) related to guest satisfaction, check-in efficiency, and problem resolution.

- ○ **Regular Performance Reviews**: Periodic performance reviews are crucial for identifying strengths, areas for improvement, and career development opportunities. Constructive feedback helps employees grow professionally and enhances the overall performance of the team.

Scheduling and Managing Shifts

1. **Importance of Efficient Scheduling**:

  o **Balancing Workload**: Proper scheduling ensures that the front office is adequately staffed during peak times while also avoiding overstaffing during quieter periods. This helps maintain a high level of service without exceeding budgeted labor costs.

  o **Staff Availability and Preferences**: Scheduling should take into account individual staff preferences, availability, and workload capacity to prevent burnout and ensure that employees are working in roles suited to their strengths.

  o **Flexibility**: Offering flexibility in scheduling can improve employee satisfaction and retention. For example, allowing staff to swap shifts or offering split shifts can accommodate personal commitments and work-life balance.

2. **Managing Shift Changes and Overlaps**:

o **Shift Handover Procedures**: Effective communication between shifts is critical. Front office staff must ensure smooth handovers of guest information, special requests, and pending issues. This ensures that no guest concern goes unaddressed and that operations remain efficient.

o **Minimizing Shift Gaps**: Ensuring that there are no gaps in staffing during critical periods (such as early check-ins or check-out times) is crucial to prevent delays and ensure guests are attended to promptly.

3. **Use of Scheduling Software**:

o Many hotels use scheduling software to manage front office staff shifts more effectively. These systems allow managers to create and adjust schedules easily, track staff hours, and ensure compliance with labor regulations.

o Scheduling software can also help managers identify trends in guest arrivals and departures, allowing for more accurate staffing projections based on occupancy forecasts.

Importance of Teamwork and Leadership in the Front Office

1. **Teamwork in the Front Office:**

   o **Collaborative Approach**: Successful front office operations depend on effective teamwork. Front desk agents, concierge staff, bellhops, housekeeping, and other hotel departments must work together seamlessly to deliver a smooth guest experience.

- o **Communication**: Clear and constant communication is essential for teamwork. Front office staff must communicate with other departments to address guest requests, resolve issues, and ensure all aspects of the guest's stay are handled efficiently.

- o **Shared Responsibility**: Every team member should understand that they are part of a larger effort to create the best possible experience for guests. A collaborative attitude fosters mutual respect and encourages staff to help one another, especially during peak times.

2. **Leadership in the Front Office**:

- o **Leading by Example**: Effective leadership involves setting a positive example for the team. Front office managers and supervisors should model professional behavior, demonstrate excellent customer service, and show a strong work ethic, setting a standard for staff to follow.

o **Providing Guidance and Support**: Good leaders in the front office provide guidance to staff, offering support during challenging situations. They should be available to assist with difficult guest interactions, resolve conflicts, and ensure that staff feel empowered to perform their roles confidently.

o **Mentorship and Development**: Effective leaders act as mentors, helping employees develop professionally and providing opportunities for career advancement.

By fostering an environment of growth and learning, leaders can retain talented staff and enhance team morale.

o **Conflict Resolution**: Leaders must handle any interpersonal conflicts within the team promptly and fairly. Addressing issues head-on ensures a positive work environment where staff feel supported and valued.

Managing front office staff is a dynamic and ongoing process that requires careful attention to recruitment, training, scheduling, and fostering teamwork. A customer-focused approach and strong leadership can elevate the performance of front office staff, resulting in improved guest experiences, higher employee morale, and smoother operations. By developing a well-trained, motivated, and cohesive team, front office managers can drive the success of the hotel and ensure that guests receive the highest level of service.

Chapter 15: Revenue Management and Front Office

Revenue management is a crucial aspect of hotel operations, especially in the front office, where the interaction with guests directly influences pricing, booking decisions, and occupancy rates. This chapter delves into the fundamentals of revenue management in the front office, including dynamic pricing, strategies for maximizing revenue and occupancy, and how the front office collaborates with the sales team for group reservations.

Basics of Revenue Management in the Front Office

1. **What is Revenue Management?**

   o Revenue management in the hotel industry is the practice of optimizing room rates and occupancy to maximize overall revenue. It involves forecasting demand, setting pricing strategies, and adjusting rates based on market conditions, guest profiles, and booking patterns.

o The front office plays a key role in revenue management as it directly impacts room rates, availability, and booking decisions. Front desk agents often interact with guests regarding reservations, upgrades, and cancellations, which makes them integral to implementing revenue management strategies.

2. **The Role of the Front Office in Revenue Management**:

   o **Pricing and Availability Control**: Front office managers and staff are responsible for ensuring that room rates are in line with the hotel's revenue strategy. They adjust pricing based on occupancy forecasts, demand, and competitor analysis.

- o **Upselling and Cross-Selling**: Front office staff often have the opportunity to upsell premium rooms or services (e.g., spa treatments, dining, upgrades) to guests during check-in or reservation interactions. This is a direct way to increase revenue per guest.

- o **Guest Segmentation**: The front office can assist in segmenting guests based on characteristics like business or leisure travel, loyalty status, and booking source, helping to adjust strategies and provide personalized offers. Understanding different guest segments allows for better pricing and offers tailored to each group.

3. **The Importance of Forecasting and Analysis**:

o Front office managers and teams need to regularly forecast demand based on historical data, seasonal trends, and upcoming events in the area. By analyzing occupancy patterns, booking lead times, and booking channels, the front office can anticipate fluctuations in demand and adjust room rates accordingly.

Dynamic Pricing and Room Rate Strategies

1. What is Dynamic Pricing?

o Dynamic pricing refers to the practice of adjusting room rates based on real-time demand, market conditions, and guest behavior. The goal is to maximize revenue by selling rooms at the highest price possible when demand is high, and at a competitive price when demand is lower.

o **Factors Affecting Dynamic Pricing**:

- **Demand Fluctuations**: Room prices should reflect changes in demand, such as high demand during holidays or events versus slower periods like mid-week or off-season.

- **Competitor Analysis**: Prices should be adjusted in response to competitor pricing strategies, ensuring the hotel remains competitive within the market while maximizing its own revenue.

- **Length of Stay**: Discounts for longer stays, or higher rates for short-term stays, can help optimize revenue and encourage guests to book for extended periods.

2. **Revenue Management Tools and Software**:

- Many hotels use sophisticated software tools to automate dynamic pricing, which adjusts room rates based on algorithms that take into account demand, competitor rates, historical data, and other market factors. These tools also provide front office staff with real-time pricing updates and suggestions for adjustments.

- **Revenue Management Systems (RMS)** are designed to analyze and predict booking trends, occupancy levels, and room pricing, enabling front office managers to make data-driven decisions to maximize revenue.

3. **Price Optimization Strategies**:

- **Barriers and Restrictions**: Implementing price floors (minimum prices) and price ceilings (maximum prices) ensures that rates remain within acceptable ranges for guests and for profitability. This prevents rooms from being sold too cheaply during high-demand periods.

o **Discount Strategies**: Offering early-bird discounts or last-minute deals based on demand forecasts can help fill rooms during slower periods. However, these should be strategically used to avoid undermining the overall pricing strategy.

Techniques for Maximizing Occupancy and Revenue

1. **Overbooking Strategy**:

   o Overbooking is a common practice in revenue management where a hotel books more reservations than it has available rooms. This strategy compensates for potential cancellations and no-shows, helping to ensure maximum occupancy.

o **Risk Management**: While overbooking can increase revenue, it carries the risk of having to turn away guests. Front office staff should be trained to manage these situations effectively, ensuring guest satisfaction even if alternative accommodations need to be arranged.

o **Cancellation Policies**: Clear and consistent cancellation policies can help mitigate the risks associated with overbooking. The front office must communicate these policies to guests and ensure they are upheld.

2. **Maximizing Revenue per Available Room (RevPAR)**:

o **RevPAR** is a key performance metric that combines room occupancy and average daily rate (ADR). Increasing RevPAR is a direct goal of revenue management strategies.

o Front office teams can contribute to this by maximizing the number of rooms sold at the best possible rates. Strategies include adjusting pricing based on demand, offering package deals (e.g., room + breakfast or room + spa), and implementing up-sell and cross-sell techniques at check-in.

3. **Maximizing Occupancy**:

o **Effective Distribution Channels**: Front office staff must ensure rooms are available on all relevant distribution channels (online travel agents, direct bookings, global distribution systems, etc.) to increase visibility and bookings.

- **Managing Walk-ins and No-shows**: The front office team should track walk-in guests and adjust availability accordingly. Efficiently managing no-shows and cancellations can prevent rooms from sitting empty.

- **Loyalty Programs**: Encouraging guests to book directly through the hotel's loyalty program can help increase occupancy while avoiding commission fees to third-party booking sites. Front office staff can promote loyalty benefits during check-in and reservations.

Working with the Sales Team for Group Reservations

1. **Collaboration with Sales**:

   - The front office must work closely with the sales team to manage group bookings and block reservations effectively. Group reservations are often made in advance, requiring special pricing and coordination to ensure smooth check-in and guest accommodation.

o **Group Discounts and Negotiation**: Sales teams negotiate group rates based on the number of rooms booked, length of stay, and other factors. The front office helps implement these rates and ensures that the group booking process is seamless.

o **Handling Special Requests for Groups**: Front office staff must coordinate with the sales team to ensure that any special requests from group leaders (e.g., room configurations, banquet services) are met. This collaboration ensures that both the sales team and front office are aligned in delivering a positive experience for group guests.

2. **Group Arrival and Departure Coordination**:

- o **Check-in and Check-out Procedures**: Group check-ins and check-outs are more complex than individual ones. The front office team must ensure that group members are processed quickly and accurately, often preparing in advance by blocking rooms together and issuing group keys.

- o **Ensuring Smooth Operations**: To manage the flow of guests, the front office must coordinate with other departments (e.g., housekeeping, catering, concierge) to ensure that group members' needs are met without delays, such as ensuring rooms are ready ahead of time, arranging transportation, or coordinating meal times.

3. **Tracking Group Performance**:

o The front office, along with the sales team, should monitor group performance, analyzing factors such as revenue generated, occupancy, and any specific needs or challenges that arose during the stay. This feedback helps refine future group booking strategies and identify opportunities for upselling or improving the guest experience.

Revenue management is a critical function for the front office, and its successful implementation can significantly impact a hotel's profitability. By utilizing dynamic pricing, maximizing occupancy, and collaborating closely with the sales team on group reservations, the front office team can play an essential role in driving revenue growth. Understanding the principles of revenue management, from forecasting demand to optimizing room rates and occupancy, is key to ensuring that the hotel remains competitive in the market while delivering exceptional value to guests.

Chapter 16: Housekeeping Coordination with Front Office

Effective coordination between the front office and housekeeping is essential for the smooth operation of any hotel. The seamless collaboration between these two departments ensures that rooms are clean, ready, and available for guests, creating a positive guest experience. This chapter explores the importance of communication between the front office and housekeeping, how room status and occupancy are coordinated, and the procedures for handling guest room requests, special instructions, and inspections.

Importance of Communication Between Front Office and Housekeeping

1. **Centralized Communication**:

- The front office and housekeeping departments must maintain open and continuous lines of communication. Information regarding guest check-ins, check-outs, room changes, and requests needs to be shared in real time to ensure that rooms are available, clean, and prepared according to guest expectations.

- Communication can take place through various methods: daily briefing meetings, internal communication systems, or property management software. It's essential to keep all staff informed about occupancy levels, special requests, and room statuses to prevent miscommunication.

2. **Impact on Guest Experience**:

- The primary goal of both departments is to provide a seamless experience for guests. Delays or errors in communication, such as assigning an unclean room to a guest, can result in dissatisfaction, complaints, and even lost business. By working together efficiently, both departments help prevent such issues, improving overall guest satisfaction and operational efficiency.

o A cooperative working relationship between the front office and housekeeping can also foster a positive work environment, ensuring a motivated team that works toward common goals of service excellence and guest satisfaction.

3. **Consistency and Accountability**:

o Clear communication sets expectations, making it easier to track the status of rooms and guest requests. Both departments need to hold each other accountable to ensure that the right information reaches the right people at the right time. Front office staff rely on housekeeping to update room statuses promptly, and housekeeping needs the front office to relay guest information, check-out times, and special requests accurately.

Room Status and Occupancy Coordination

1. **Room Status Updates**:

   o **Room Ready**: A key part of the front office and housekeeping communication is the real-time update of room status. When a guest checks in, the front office must be aware of which rooms are cleaned, inspected, and ready for occupancy. Housekeeping should inform the front office as soon as rooms are prepared, while the front office should promptly relay guest arrivals and special needs (e.g., early check-ins).

- ○ **Stay-Over, Vacant, and Check-Out Rooms**: Room status tracking should include the following key categories:

  - ▪ **Stay-over Rooms**: Rooms that are occupied but will not be checked out by the guest on the same day.

  - ▪ **Vacant Rooms**: Rooms that are empty and require cleaning.

  - ▪ **Check-out Rooms**: Rooms that will become vacant after a guest's departure and need to be cleaned.

- ○ **Real-Time Updates**: A well-functioning communication system, such as a property management system (PMS), enables real-time updates for both front office and housekeeping, ensuring accuracy and reducing errors. If a guest checks out earlier than expected or requests a late check-out, the front office needs to inform housekeeping to adjust their cleaning schedule accordingly.

2. **Occupancy Forecasting**:

o Accurate room status reporting is crucial for occupancy forecasting. By communicating occupancy levels, the front office can plan for guest arrivals, check-ins, and expected departures. Housekeeping staff can adjust their cleaning schedules based on the forecast to ensure that rooms are ready and clean when required.

o A sudden surge in occupancy (e.g., due to last-minute bookings or extended stays) requires flexibility in housekeeping's ability to prepare rooms on short notice. The front office needs to communicate this need promptly to ensure that housekeeping can allocate resources efficiently.

Handling Guest Room Requests and Special Instructions

1. **Special Requests**:

    o Guests often have specific preferences or needs that must be communicated between the front office and housekeeping, such as room preferences (e.g., near the elevator, away from the street), extra towels, pillows, or specific amenities. Ensuring that these requests are passed along accurately and promptly helps to create a more personalized guest experience.

    o **Guest Arrival**: Before guest check-in, the front office should provide housekeeping with any specific guest requests or preferences. For example, if a guest requires a hypoallergenic room, additional amenities, or a baby crib, the front office should relay this information well in advance.

- **Guest Departure**: At check-out, the front office may inform housekeeping of any additional needs or guest feedback, such as complaints or special thank-you notes. This provides housekeeping staff with the opportunity to address concerns before the next guest arrives.

2. **Handling VIP and Special Guests**:

- VIPs, frequent guests, or guests with special needs may have specific requirements. Front office staff need to communicate these preferences to housekeeping for special treatment, such as ensuring a suite is ready in advance, setting up additional amenities, or providing specific services. A VIP guest might expect a certain level of room presentation or personalized touches, which should be communicated and respected.

o Housekeeping should also be aware of any high-priority rooms and prioritize their cleaning and inspection. Both departments need to coordinate to ensure that the guest's needs are met before and during their stay.

3. **Coordination for Specific Needs**:

   o **Early Check-ins and Late Check-outs**: When a guest requests an early check-in or late check-out, the front office should notify housekeeping accordingly. Early check-ins may require rooms to be cleaned ahead of time, while late check-outs could require room extensions or cleaning deferrals. Effective communication between departments helps manage these situations smoothly.

○ **Maintenance Requests**: If a guest reports an issue with their room (e.g., a broken light, malfunctioning air conditioning), the front office should immediately inform housekeeping or maintenance to address the problem. Housekeeping can inspect the issue, or the maintenance team can prioritize it, ensuring that the room is restored to its proper condition for the next guest.

Procedures for Room Inspections and Readiness

1. **Room Inspection**:

○ **Pre-Arrival Inspections**: Before a guest checks in, housekeeping should conduct a thorough inspection of the room to ensure it is clean, well-maintained, and equipped with all necessary amenities. Once the room is cleaned and ready, the housekeeping supervisor or designated staff member should conduct a final inspection. The room is only marked as "ready for occupancy" when it passes this inspection.

o **Quality Control**: The front office needs to have a clear understanding of room inspection standards. If a room is not up to the expected quality, the front office should be notified so they can adjust room assignments or communicate the delay to guests waiting for check-in.

2. **Real-Time Readiness Updates**:

o **Communication of Room Status**: When rooms are ready, housekeeping should promptly update the front office with this information. Any delays in cleaning or inspection should be communicated immediately to adjust guest expectations and avoid inconvenience.

o **Handling Urgent Room Requests**: For urgent requests, such as VIP or high-priority guests, front office staff should alert housekeeping to fast-track room preparation. Housekeeping should be flexible in such instances, ensuring that the room is quickly cleaned and inspected for guest use.

3. **Post-Check-Out Room Inspections**:

o **Final Inspections**: After a guest checks out, housekeeping is responsible for cleaning and inspecting the room. This includes ensuring that the room is free of any lost or left-behind items, the cleanliness meets standards, and the room is set up for the next guest. The front office needs to be notified when the room is ready for the next guest to be assigned.

Housekeeping and front office coordination is essential to the success of any hotel, as it directly impacts guest satisfaction, operational efficiency, and revenue. Clear communication between the two departments ensures that rooms are clean, ready, and available according to guest needs, contributing to a seamless guest experience. Effective coordination not only minimizes errors and delays but also maximizes efficiency and creates an environment where both staff and guests are happy. By following well-established procedures for room status updates, handling guest requests, and ensuring room readiness, both departments can work together to provide a superior hospitality experience.

Chapter 17: Marketing and Sales Coordination

In the hospitality industry, the front office plays a vital role not just in guest services but also in driving hotel revenue through effective marketing and sales coordination. This chapter explores how the front office collaborates with the marketing and sales departments to promote hotel services, upsell add-on offerings, manage VIP guests, and support promotional activities. By aligning with these departments, the front office contributes to enhancing the guest experience while maximizing revenue.

Role of the Front Office in Marketing Hotel Services

1. **Front Office as the Brand Ambassador**:

   o The front office is often the first point of contact for guests, making it a key player in conveying the hotel's brand and services. Front office staff must be well-versed in the hotel's offerings, promotions, and unique selling points to effectively market these to guests.

- o **Service Promotion**: When guests check in, the front office can promote on-site services like dining, spa treatments, room upgrades, or special events. Staff should be trained to highlight the benefits of these services to encourage guests to make additional bookings during their stay.

- o **Guest Engagement**: Front office staff can engage guests with personalized recommendations for services based on their preferences or the purpose of their stay. For example, business travelers may appreciate information about meeting rooms or express laundry, while leisure travelers may be interested in local tours or recreational activities offered by the hotel.

2. **Leveraging Hotel Amenities and Features**:

o The front office should emphasize the amenities available at the hotel (e.g., fitness center, pool, conference rooms, concierge services) and explain how they enhance the guest experience. By effectively communicating the hotel's unique features, front office staff can promote both on-site services and additional revenue-generating options.

o **Cross-Promotions**: Front office staff can collaborate with the marketing team to offer cross-promotions, such as combining room rates with packages (e.g., bed-and-breakfast deals, spa packages) or promoting limited-time discounts for in-house services.

Promoting Upsells and Add-on Services

1. **Understanding Upselling**:

o Upselling involves encouraging guests to purchase more expensive rooms or services than initially booked, improving the guest experience while increasing revenue for the hotel. Front office staff are ideally positioned to promote room upgrades, premium services, and additional amenities when guests arrive or during their stay.

o **Room Upgrades**: A key area where the front office plays a significant role is in offering room upgrades, such as moving a guest to a higher category room or a suite with additional amenities. This should be done based on availability, guest preferences, and loyalty status. Offering an upgrade at check-in is a great way to enhance the guest experience while increasing revenue.

o **Add-on Services**: These include promoting services such as breakfast, airport transfers, spa treatments, guided tours, early check-ins, late check-outs, and premium internet access. The front office staff can highlight these services during check-in or through direct communication channels like the hotel app or guest emails.

2. **Timing and Personalization of Offers**:

o Effective upselling is about timing and personalizing offers. Front office agents should be trained to listen to guest needs and suggest the most relevant services at the right time. For example, if a guest mentions they're celebrating a special occasion, the front office could offer a bottle of champagne or a romantic dinner package. Tailored offers resonate more with guests and lead to higher conversion rates.

- **Incentive Programs**: Some hotels use incentive-based programs where front office staff are rewarded for successful upselling. This creates motivation and reinforces the importance of upselling to staff.

3. **Promoting Loyalty Programs**:

- Loyalty programs are essential for increasing repeat business. The front office should actively promote the hotel's loyalty program to guests, especially at check-in. Front office agents should explain the benefits, such as earning points for future stays, exclusive discounts, or access to VIP perks.

- **Guest Enrollment**: The front office team is responsible for enrolling new guests into the loyalty program and encouraging existing guests to sign up or maintain their membership. They should ensure that members receive any applicable benefits, such as room upgrades or early check-in.

o **Reward Redemption**: Front office staff should also assist guests in redeeming loyalty points for free nights, upgrades, or other amenities. Clear communication of the available rewards and easy redemption processes help foster positive guest relationships and loyalty.

Handling VIP Guests and Loyalty Programs

1. **VIP Guest Management**:

   o VIP guests, including repeat customers, high-profile clients, or those in loyalty programs, often require special attention and personalized services. The front office plays a key role in recognizing and catering to these guests by ensuring their specific needs and preferences are met.

o **Personalized Service**: For VIP guests, the front office should provide personalized check-in experiences, including welcoming them with special amenities (e.g., complimentary drinks, flowers, or notes), assigning their preferred rooms, and prioritizing their requests. It's crucial for front office staff to anticipate needs based on the guest's history and preferences to enhance their stay.

o **VIP Benefits**: VIP guests should receive exclusive perks such as expedited check-in/check-out, priority room service, access to lounges, or complimentary services. These benefits should be communicated clearly during the check-in process.

2. **Tracking and Recognizing Loyal Guests**:

o The front office should be equipped with systems to track VIP status and loyalty membership so that staff can immediately recognize these guests and provide tailored services. A guest's loyalty status should be flagged in the property management system (PMS), allowing front office agents to personalize their interactions and ensure VIP guests are consistently given priority treatment.

o **Special Requests and Expectations**: Front office staff should be aware of the unique needs of loyal and VIP guests, which could include dietary preferences, room configurations, or additional services. Maintaining a guest profile with this information ensures that the hotel can deliver a seamless experience upon every visit.

Working with the Sales Department for Promotional Activities

1. **Collaborating on Promotional Campaigns**:

   o Front office staff should be well-informed about ongoing marketing promotions, special packages, and sales campaigns so they can communicate these effectively to guests. Whether it's a limited-time offer or a seasonal package, the front office serves as the on-the-ground team to promote these campaigns during guest interactions.

   o **Cross-Department Coordination**: The front office needs to work closely with the sales and marketing departments to align messaging, offer details, and target specific customer segments. Sales teams can share information on group bookings or upcoming events that may influence room occupancy, which can help the front office tailor promotional offers.

o **Promotional Materials**: Sales and marketing teams often provide the front office with promotional brochures, flyers, or digital content to distribute to guests. Front desk agents should be trained to present these materials effectively during check-in or upon guest inquiry.

2. **Special Offers and Discounts**:

o Front office staff can be key to driving the success of promotional offers, such as limited-time discounts, early-bird specials, or stay-and-save packages. These offers should be clearly communicated to guests, especially when they are booking directly with the hotel.

o **Up-selling Promotions**: Sales teams may create bundled packages (e.g., stay two nights, get one free, or room + dining) that the front office can promote during check-in or at other touchpoints. By offering these promotions, front office staff can increase ancillary revenue while providing value to guests.

3. **Event and Group Booking Promotions**:

o When group bookings or events are planned, the front office must coordinate with the sales department to ensure that promotional offers are extended to those guests. For example, conference attendees may be offered discounted rates or package deals for additional services (e.g., catering, meeting rooms, and entertainment).

o **Group Reservations**: The front office works closely with the sales team to ensure that group reservations are processed smoothly, that all rooms are allocated properly, and that the group receives any promotional rates or additional services that have been agreed upon.

The front office plays a critical role in hotel marketing and sales, acting as the direct interface between the hotel and its guests. By promoting hotel services, upselling, managing VIP guests, and collaborating with the sales team for promotional activities, the front office contributes not only to enhancing guest satisfaction but also to increasing hotel revenue. Effective marketing and sales coordination require constant communication, a solid understanding of guest needs, and a proactive approach to upselling and promotions. By aligning the front office's efforts with the sales and marketing strategy, hotels can create a more profitable and guest-centric environment.

Chapter 18: Guest Feedback and Service Improvement

Guest feedback is a cornerstone of hospitality excellence. By actively seeking, analyzing, and responding to guest input, hotels can continuously improve their services, create memorable guest experiences, and foster loyalty. This chapter delves into how the front office can collect and utilize guest feedback, the importance of analyzing it for service enhancement, and how ongoing training and improvements help maintain high standards of service.

Collecting Guest Feedback

1. **In-Person Feedback**:

   o **Personal Interaction**: One of the most effective ways to collect feedback is through direct, in-person communication. Front office staff, especially at check-out or during guest interactions at the desk, can ask guests about their experience. Open-ended questions such as "How was your stay?" or "Is there anything we can improve?" provide valuable insights. Front office personnel should be trained to approach guests with genuine interest in their feedback.

- **During Service Delivery**: As guests interact with the front office for various services (e.g., reservations, check-ins, concierge assistance), staff should subtly prompt feedback. For example, when assisting with special requests or handling complaints, front office agents can ask how the guest feels about the resolution or service, ensuring that feedback is collected throughout the guest's stay.

○ **Exit Surveys**: The final opportunity to collect feedback comes when guests check out. Front desk staff can ask guests to participate in a quick survey or fill out a short feedback form. This approach allows the hotel to capture immediate impressions from the guest before they leave.

2. **Digital Surveys and Online Feedback**:

○ **Automated Surveys**: Digital surveys are increasingly popular as a convenient method of collecting guest feedback. After check-out, guests can be sent an email or SMS asking them to rate their experience. These surveys can cover a range of topics, such as the quality of service, cleanliness, staff behavior, and amenities. Using platforms like email surveys, third-party booking sites (e.g., TripAdvisor, Booking.com), and hotel apps, hotels can easily collect feedback in a timely manner.

- o **Social Media and Review Sites**: Guests may also provide feedback through social media or review sites. Hotels should encourage guests to share their experiences on platforms like Google Reviews, Yelp, or the hotel's social media pages. Engaging with guest reviews on these platforms demonstrates attentiveness and willingness to improve based on feedback. Front office staff can direct satisfied guests to leave positive reviews, while also addressing any complaints left online.

- o **Guest Feedback Kiosks**: Some hotels use in-house feedback kiosks in high-traffic areas, such as the lobby, where guests can quickly rate their experience. These can be a more immediate form of collecting feedback and may encourage guests to voice their opinions in real-time.

Analyzing Guest Feedback for Service Improvement

1. **Identifying Common Trends and Issues**:

   o **Quantitative and Qualitative Data**: Guest feedback often comes in two forms: quantitative (ratings or scores) and qualitative (written comments). Front office teams must ensure both types of feedback are carefully reviewed. Quantitative data is easy to measure and provides clear insights into overall guest satisfaction, while qualitative feedback offers detailed context and deeper understanding.

   o **Tracking Patterns**: Regularly analyzing feedback helps identify recurring trends or issues that may require attention. For example, if multiple guests mention issues with room cleanliness or slow check-in procedures, these are areas that should be prioritized for improvement. Grouping feedback by categories such as room quality, staff performance, amenities, and service speed can help target specific areas for improvement.

2. **Use of Technology for Analysis**:

o Many hotels use guest feedback management software that collects and organizes data from various sources, such as surveys, online reviews, and social media. This software can automatically analyze sentiment (positive, negative, or neutral) and create reports to help identify key areas where service may need to be improved.

- o **Benchmarking**: Comparing feedback to industry standards or competitors' reviews can help the hotel assess how well it is performing in comparison to others. If guests rate the hotel lower on specific aspects like service speed or cleanliness compared to competitors, it signals areas for improvement.

3. **Engagement with Guests**:

- o Front office staff should not only collect and analyze feedback but also engage with guests to acknowledge their concerns and thank them for their input. When responding to feedback, it's essential to convey that the hotel values the guest's opinion and is committed to continuous improvement.

o **Follow-Up on Complaints**: When guests leave feedback regarding complaints or dissatisfaction, it's important for the front office to follow up with them to resolve the issue. In some cases, offering compensation (e.g., a discount, complimentary service, or future discounts) can help recover the guest's trust and encourage repeat visits.

Implementing Changes Based on Guest Insights

1. **Prioritizing Actionable Feedback**:

   o Not all feedback can be immediately addressed, but it's crucial to act on those comments that can lead to a direct improvement in the guest experience. For example, if multiple guests complain about uncomfortable beds, this would be an area to prioritize for improvement, as it directly impacts guest satisfaction.

o Changes should be communicated clearly to the entire team, including housekeeping, maintenance, and food and beverage departments, so everyone is aligned in making improvements that will have the most significant impact on guest satisfaction.

2. **Service Improvements and Adjustments**:

o **Training and Development**: Guest feedback often highlights areas where staff performance may need improvement. For example, if guests consistently rate the staff's responsiveness as low, this can be addressed through additional training on customer service, conflict resolution, and communication skills. Providing staff with the tools and knowledge they need to improve service is key to ensuring that feedback leads to positive changes.

- **Operational Changes**: In addition to training, operational changes may be necessary. If guests are complaining about long wait times at check-in, for example, the front office may introduce a faster check-in process, implement self-check-in kiosks, or improve staff scheduling to ensure there are enough agents available during peak times.

- **Facility and Amenities Updates**: Feedback may point to issues with hotel facilities or amenities. For example, if guests frequently comment on outdated furniture, noisy air conditioning, or inadequate lighting in rooms, management may prioritize updating these aspects. Regularly investing in facility upgrades and ensuring that the property remains modern and functional is critical for maintaining guest satisfaction.

3. **Continuous Improvement Process**:

- o Feedback collection and analysis should be an ongoing process. Once changes are made, it's important to continue gathering feedback to assess whether these changes have had a positive effect. This helps to create a cycle of continuous improvement, where service standards are continually raised based on the evolving needs of guests.

- o **Guest Feedback Loops**: Establishing a guest feedback loop is essential in keeping guests informed of changes that have been made based on their input. This could involve sending an email or posting updates on the hotel website or social media.

Acknowledging that guest feedback has led to improvements shows guests that their opinions truly matter and that the hotel is committed to providing the best possible service.

Importance of Continuous Training and Improvement

1. **Employee Training**:

   o Continuous training for front office staff is crucial for maintaining high service standards. Regular training sessions help employees stay updated on best practices, new technologies, and the latest trends in hospitality. Front office staff should be trained not only in their technical skills but also in soft skills like communication, empathy, and problem-solving to handle guest concerns effectively.

o **Guest Experience Training**: Training should focus on creating an exceptional guest experience by anticipating guest needs, addressing complaints, and turning negative experiences into positive ones. Front office staff should be equipped with strategies to handle various situations, from managing difficult guests to resolving service issues.

2. **Empowering Staff to Act on Feedback**:

o Front office staff should be empowered to act on guest feedback promptly. This means giving employees the authority to make decisions and implement small service changes without always needing managerial approval. Empowering staff to take ownership of guest concerns creates a more responsive, guest-centered culture.

o **Performance Reviews**: Regular performance reviews based on guest feedback can help staff understand their strengths and areas for improvement. Recognizing and rewarding employees who excel in guest satisfaction can motivate others to enhance their performance.

Guest feedback is an invaluable resource for hotel management and staff. By collecting feedback from various channels, analyzing it for trends and areas for improvement, and implementing actionable changes, the front office can continuously enhance the guest experience. Coupled with ongoing staff training, a culture of service excellence, and proactive problem-solving, feedback collection becomes a powerful tool for driving service improvements and maintaining guest loyalty. By using guest feedback as a guide, hotels can remain competitive, deliver exceptional service, and ensure that each guest's experience is better than the last.

Chapter 19: Financial and Statistical Analysis for Front Office

In the hospitality industry, the front office plays a crucial role not just in guest services but also in contributing to the financial success of the hotel. This chapter explores the financial and statistical aspects of front office operations, including key performance indicators (KPIs), budgeting, forecasting, and the analysis of occupancy and revenue statistics. Proper analysis and reporting are essential for monitoring performance, identifying trends, and making data-driven decisions that can enhance both guest satisfaction and profitability.

Key Performance Indicators (KPIs) for the Front Office

1. **Overview of KPIs in Front Office**:

   o **KPIs** are metrics used to evaluate the success of various front office operations and how effectively they contribute to the hotel's overall performance. KPIs help identify strengths, highlight areas for improvement, and support decision-making.

o Front office KPIs typically focus on guest satisfaction, operational efficiency, and financial performance. By tracking these KPIs, the front office can contribute to achieving broader business goals.

2. **Common KPIs for Front Office**:

o **Occupancy Rate**: This is the percentage of rooms occupied during a given period. A high occupancy rate indicates the hotel is effectively filling its rooms and can generate more revenue.

o **Average Daily Rate (ADR)**: ADR measures the average rate per occupied room. It provides insight into pricing strategies and the hotel's ability to maximize room rates.

o **Revenue per Available Room (RevPAR)**: RevPAR is a key performance metric that combines occupancy rate and ADR. It is calculated by multiplying the ADR by the occupancy rate, providing a comprehensive measure of room revenue generation.

o **Guest Satisfaction Score (GSS)**: This metric measure guest satisfaction based on feedback, surveys, and reviews. High guest satisfaction correlates with repeat business, positive reviews, and higher loyalty.

o **Length of Stay (LOS)**: This metric indicates how long guests stay at the hotel. Longer stays contribute more to revenue and may reduce the cost per guest for the hotel.

○ **Check-in and Check-out Time Efficiency**: This KPI tracks the speed and efficiency of the check-in/check-out process. Faster times lead to improved guest satisfaction and better operational flow.

○ **Employee Productivity**: This KPI measures the efficiency of front office staff in relation to guest service and revenue generation. It includes metrics such as the number of rooms processed per front desk agent per shift or the number of phone calls handled.

3. **Monitoring KPIs for Performance Management**:

○ **Trend Analysis**: By tracking KPIs over time, the front office can identify trends, such as seasonal fluctuations or shifts in guest behavior. For instance, if occupancy rates are decreasing, the front office can investigate whether pricing strategies, marketing efforts, or seasonal factors are influencing demand.

○ **Benchmarking**: Comparing the hotel's KPIs with industry standards or competitors' performance can provide insights into its relative performance. This allows the front office to identify gaps and implement corrective actions.

Budgeting and Forecasting for Front Office Operations

1. **Importance of Budgeting and Forecasting**:

   ○ Budgeting and forecasting are essential financial management tools for the front office. They allow the department to plan for expected revenue, manage costs, and allocate resources effectively to meet operational needs and financial goals.

o Accurate forecasting helps the hotel prepare for fluctuations in occupancy and revenue, ensuring that staff levels, marketing activities, and operational budgets align with demand.

2. **Budgeting for the Front Office**:

o **Revenue Budgeting**: The front office must forecast revenue from room bookings, including expected occupancy, average room rates, and ancillary services such as late check-out fees, upgrades, and early check-in charges. This budget should also account for special promotions, group bookings, and seasonal trends.

- o **Operating Expense Budget**: The front office has operational costs, including salaries, training, amenities for guests (e.g., welcome gifts, toiletries), office supplies, technology infrastructure (Property Management Systems, communication systems), and marketing expenses. These should be estimated and planned within the budget.

- o **Labor Costs**: Since the front office is a labor-intensive department, payroll and staffing levels are key considerations. The budget should forecast labor costs based on expected occupancy, seasonal variations, and projected demand for services.

3. **Forecasting for the Front Office**:

- o **Revenue Forecasting**: Forecasting revenue is critical to predict financial performance. The front office should use historical data, trends, and external factors (e.g., upcoming events, holidays, market conditions) to project occupancy and ADR.

- o **Demand and Occupancy Forecasting**: Understanding demand patterns is essential for accurate forecasting. Historical booking data can help predict periods of high or low demand, allowing the front office to adjust staffing levels and pricing strategies accordingly.

- o **Room Availability and Overbooking Forecasting**: By forecasting room availability, the front office can anticipate overbooking situations, manage reservations efficiently, and minimize the risk of guest dissatisfaction.

4. **Tools and Techniques for Forecasting**:

- o **Historical Data**: Historical data provides a strong foundation for forecasting, helping the front office predict demand based on past occupancy patterns, seasonality, and local events.

- o **PMS and Revenue Management Tools**: Property Management Systems (PMS) and revenue management software are powerful tools for forecasting and tracking key financial and operational data. These systems analyze historical trends, booking patterns, and real-time data to provide accurate revenue projections.

Analysis of Occupancy and Revenue Statistics

1. **Occupancy Analysis**:

   - o **Tracking Occupancy Levels**: By monitoring daily, weekly, and monthly occupancy rates, the front office can assess how well the hotel is utilizing its available rooms. High occupancy indicates strong demand, while low occupancy may signal the need for targeted marketing or pricing adjustments.

- o **Occupancy by Market Segment**: Analyzing occupancy by market segment (e.g., leisure, business, corporate, groups) provides insights into which guest types are driving demand. This information helps the front office tailor its marketing strategies and adjust pricing for different segments.

2. **Revenue Analysis**:

- o **ADR and RevPAR Analysis**: The front office should track ADR and RevPAR to gauge how effectively the hotel is generating revenue from room sales. A higher ADR suggests that the hotel is successfully implementing premium pricing strategies, while a high RevPAR indicates the hotel is efficiently utilizing its available rooms.

- o **Revenue by Department**: In addition to room revenue, the front office should analyze revenue generated from other departments, such as food and beverage, laundry services, and concierge. This comprehensive analysis provides a clearer picture of overall hotel performance.

- o **Seasonal and Event-Driven Revenue Trends**: Revenue can fluctuate based on seasonality or special events (e.g., conferences, festivals, holidays). By analyzing historical data on these events, the front office can better forecast demand and adjust room rates accordingly.

3. **Revenue Leakage and Error Identification**:

- ○ Regular analysis helps identify revenue leakage situations where potential revenue is lost due to errors or inefficiencies. For example, mistakes in billing, missed opportunities for upselling, or errors in reservations (e.g., no-shows or cancellations not properly accounted for) can all impact revenue. The front office should implement regular audits and checks to minimize such losses.

- ○ **Inventory Control and Revenue Optimization**: The front office should monitor room inventory to ensure that rooms are priced appropriately based on demand. Underpricing during high demand periods and overpricing during low demand can negatively affect both occupancy and revenue.

Reporting and Documenting Front Office Performance

1. **Daily Reports**:

   o Front office teams should compile and distribute daily reports that summarize key performance data. These reports typically include occupancy rates, ADR, RevPAR, guest feedback, and financial transactions for the day. Daily reports provide management with an up-to-date snapshot of hotel performance and help ensure that any issues are addressed promptly.

   o **Revenue Reports**: These include details on room revenue, ancillary revenue, and sales from the front office. They highlight total earnings, segmented by room category, guest type, and additional services provided.

2. **Weekly and Monthly Reports**:

o **Performance Review**: Weekly and monthly reports provide a more detailed view of front office performance and are essential for evaluating trends over time. These reports can show longer-term patterns, such as changes in occupancy due to seasonal fluctuations, or the success of recent promotions or rate changes.

o **Forecast and Budget Comparison**: Monthly reports compare actual performance against budgeted revenue and occupancy forecasts. This allows management to assess whether the front office is meeting its financial targets and identify areas where corrective action may be necessary.

3. **Forecasting Adjustments**:

o If performance deviates significantly from forecasts (e.g., lower-than-expected occupancy or ADR), the front office must make adjustments. Reports should be used as a tool to revise future forecasts, update pricing strategies, and reallocate resources where necessary.

4. **Documentation of Policies and Procedures**:

○ Clear documentation of front office procedures and policies helps ensure consistent performance. This includes check-in and check-out procedures, guest service protocols, and billing practices. Detailed records of operational procedures also help during audits and in case of any financial discrepancies.

Financial and statistical analysis is an essential aspect of front office operations, ensuring that the hotel operates efficiently and remains profitable. By focusing on KPIs, budgeting, forecasting, and analyzing occupancy and revenue statistics, the front office can optimize its performance and contribute to the hotel's financial health. Regular reporting, data-driven decision-making, and ongoing performance assessments allow the front office to adjust strategies, minimize costs, and maximize revenue. Ultimately, a strong financial and statistical analysis process leads to more informed decision-making, enhanced operational efficiency, and a better overall guest experience.

Chapter 20: Front Office Trends and Future Outlook

The front office department plays a vital role in the hospitality industry, and its function is continuously evolving. In this chapter, we explore the key trends shaping the future of front office management, including technological advancements, shifting guest expectations, the impact of automation, and the increasing focus on environmental sustainability. Additionally, we will discuss the future of front office careers and the necessary skills for future professionals in this dynamic environment.

Trends in Front Office Management and Guest Expectations

1. **Increased Guest Demand for Personalization**:

   o Modern travelers are increasingly seeking personalized experiences during their stays. Guests expect hotels to understand their preferences and provide tailored services, from room choices to special amenities. This trend places a greater emphasis on the front office's ability to collect and manage guest data effectively.

   o Personalization is made possible through integrated systems that track guest preferences, previous stays, and special requests. The front office is tasked with utilizing this data to create memorable experiences, from greeting guests by name to offering customized recommendations for dining or local activities.

2. **Contactless and Self-Service Options**:

   o With the growing demand for convenience and safety, many hotels are adopting contactless check-in/check-out processes and self-service kiosks. Guests can now check in using mobile apps or kiosks, bypassing the front desk entirely. This trend not only streamlines operations but also aligns with guest preferences for minimal contact.

   o Self-service technology extends beyond check-in. Digital keys, in-room smart devices (such as controlling lighting and temperature via smartphones), and automated check-out options are becoming more commonplace. The role of the front office evolves from traditional check-ins to providing more personalized, behind-the-scenes support.

3. **Seamless Integration of Omnichannel Communication**:

   o Guests increasingly interact with the front office through various communication channels: in person, via phone, email, messaging apps, and social media. The front office must adapt to this multi-channel environment by providing seamless and consistent service across all platforms.

   o Mobile messaging platforms, chatbots, and AI-driven customer service tools are enhancing communication by allowing staff to respond quickly to guest inquiries or requests, ensuring a smooth experience for tech-savvy travelers.

4. **Elevated Guest Experience through Technology**:

   - Technology is playing a significant role in enhancing the overall guest experience. From smart rooms with voice-controlled features to virtual concierges, hotels are investing in technology to provide a more immersive and convenient stay.

   - Front office staff will need to stay ahead of these technological innovations to ensure they are equipped to guide guests in using the new technologies and troubleshooting issues when they arise.

Evolving Role of Front Office with Automation

1. **Automation in Check-in and Check-out**:

o One of the most significant trends is the automation of routine tasks such as check-in and check-out. Self-service kiosks, mobile check-in, and keyless entry systems allow guests to bypass the front desk entirely, providing faster service and minimizing wait times.

o While automation can improve efficiency, it requires the front office team to focus more on troubleshooting, handling complex requests, and offering high-level personalized services.

2. **Artificial Intelligence (AI) and Chatbots**:

o AI-powered chatbots are becoming common in the front office to handle simple tasks such as answering frequently asked questions, providing information about hotel amenities, and managing bookings. These tools enable front office staff to focus on more complex and guest-centric tasks.

o AI can also be used to predict guest preferences based on previous stays, which enhances personalization efforts and helps front office staff tailor services more effectively.

3. **Robots and Automated Concierge Services**:

o The role of robotics in the front office is growing, with robotic concierges greeting guests, delivering amenities to rooms, and even managing luggage in some hotels. These innovations improve operational efficiency and reduce staff workloads, allowing human staff to focus on more nuanced guest services.

o While robots and automation increase efficiency, it is important to maintain the human touch in the guest experience, as many travelers still value personalized interactions with front office staff.

Environmental Sustainability in Front Office Operations

1. **Green Certifications and Sustainability Initiatives**:

   o With growing awareness of environmental issues, hotels are focusing on sustainability as a key aspect of their operations. The front office is often at the forefront of promoting sustainability efforts, such as promoting eco-friendly initiatives to guests and offering incentives for reducing environmental impact (e.g., towel and linen reuse programs).

   o Sustainability also extends to waste management practices, reducing plastic usage, and adopting energy-saving technologies such as LED lighting and smart thermostats in guest rooms. Front office teams need to be knowledgeable about these efforts and communicate them to guests.

2. **Reducing Paper Usage and Embracing Digital Solutions**:

   o Digitalization in the front office extends to reducing paper usage in reservations, billing, and guest communication. Electronic invoices, digital room keys, and mobile check-ins are part of the green initiatives aimed at reducing waste and improving operational efficiency.

   o Hotels are also adopting eco-friendly practices by incorporating recycled materials in guest supplies and promotional materials. Front office staff must be trained to promote and explain these sustainability efforts to guests.

3. **Sustainability in Front Office Operations**:

   o Many hotels are implementing energy-efficient systems and using eco-friendly products. The front office, which manages guest requests and interactions, plays a role in ensuring that these sustainability practices are integrated into guest services, ensuring guests' expectations are met while also contributing to the hotel's environmental goals.

Future of Front Office Careers and Skills Development

1. **Shift in Required Skills**:

   o As technology and automation continue to shape the front office, the skillset required for front office professionals is also evolving. While traditional customer service skills will remain essential, there will be an increased emphasis on technological literacy, data analysis, and the ability to work with automated systems.

o Front office staff will need to develop competencies in managing and troubleshooting digital tools, from self-check-in kiosks to property management systems and AI-driven guest service tools.

2. **Increased Focus on Soft Skills**:

o Despite the rise in automation, soft skills such as empathy, communication, and problem-solving will remain critical to success in front office roles. Guests still value human interaction, especially in situations where issues arise, and emotional intelligence will be necessary for resolving complaints and ensuring guest satisfaction.

o Leadership, teamwork, and multitasking will continue to be key skills as front office staff work in dynamic, fast-paced environments where flexibility and adaptability are crucial.

3. **Career Development and Training**:

o As the front office becomes more technology-driven, continuous training and professional development will be essential for career progression. Front office professionals will need to stay updated with new systems and trends to remain competitive in the industry.

o Additionally, there will be more opportunities for specialized roles in revenue management, data analytics, and customer experience design, offering career paths beyond traditional front desk operations.

4. **Emphasis on Multitasking and Cross-Department Knowledge**:

  - The front office role will continue to require multitasking as staff handle multiple channels of communication, manage guest requests, and work alongside other hotel departments. Understanding the workings of various departments—housekeeping, sales, maintenance, and food and beverage—will be essential for coordinating services and enhancing the guest experience.

The future of the front office department is shaped by technological advancements, evolving guest expectations, and a greater focus on sustainability. Automation and AI are transforming routine tasks and enhancing operational efficiency, while the demand for personalization and seamless guest experiences is growing. As the industry evolves, the role of front office staff will become increasingly multifaceted, requiring new skills in technology, communication, and sustainability practices.

In the future, the front office will continue to be the cornerstone of guest relations, but the department's structure, responsibilities, and technology integration will adapt to meet the needs of a changing hospitality landscape. Front office professionals will need to stay agile, develop new competencies, and remain committed to delivering exceptional service in an increasingly automated world.

www.ingramcontent.com/pod-product-compliance
Lightning Source LLC
Chambersburg PA
CBHW072140290526
45794CB00004B/1374